The Sovereign Mindset

Unlocking Your Divine Potential

Jeremy E. McDonald

www.jeremymcdonald.net

Published by: Jeremy E. McDonald

The Sovereign Mindset – Unlocking Your Divine Potential

Author: Jeremy E. McDonald

1st Edition

Cover design © 2025 Justin Duncan

Interior design © 2025

Edited by: Linda Hinkle

ISBN: 979-8-218-80974-4

ISBN eBook: 979-8-218-80975-1

Printed in the United States of America

What people are saying about The Sovereign Mindset:

This book is more than words on a page—it is an invitation to meet yourself beyond the programs, beliefs, and patterns that have kept you small.

In *The Sovereign Mindset: Unlocking Your Divine Potential,* Jeremy McDonald offers both guidance and example: stories from his life, spiritual insights, and practical reflections that help you turn inward, where true transformation begins. This work isn't about changing your outer world—it's about the courage to dissolve what no longer serves and reconnect with the divine spark within.

What I love most is how Jeremy blends the mystical with the practical. He gives you the tools and the permission to reflect, feel, and act from a place of alignment. It's a roadmap for anyone ready to reclaim their power, step into sovereignty, and embody the fullness of their truth.

Read slowly, reflect deeply, and trust the process. The journey inward is where freedom, clarity, and your true power live.

—Cathleen Elle - Author, Speaker, Alchemy Weaver — Guiding Transformation, Truth, and Sovereign Embodiment

The Sovereign Mindset is a guide for all to learn and practice in the everyday experience of life that makes it even more profound. I have known you, Jeremy, for a long time and you speak from your heart and soul, and I am so proud to know you!

—Virginia Drake - Transformational Consultant, healer.

Jeremy has written a book that feels like sitting down with a wise friend who also happens to carry a lantern for your soul. *The Sovereign Mindset* is both gentle and empowering, weaving together stories, insights, and tools that invite us to remember who we really are—divine beings having a very human experience.

As I turned the pages, I found myself nodding, smiling, and sometimes pausing to soak in the truth that was waiting between the lines. Jeremy doesn't just write; he reminds, he reawakens, and he guides without preaching. His words feel like an open hand extended—encouraging us to release old patterns, embrace grace, and step boldly into our own sovereignty.

If you've ever longed to live with more peace, clarity, and joy—or if you've felt the nudge that there's "something more" to this life—this book will speak to you. It's not only a guide but a companion for the journey, inviting you to listen to your soul and walk forward with confidence in the light of your own divine spark.

The Sovereign Mindset is a beautiful reminder that the keys to freedom and fulfillment have always been within us, patiently waiting for us to turn them.

Kevin Lee, Spiritual Intuitive, Purpose Coach, Transformational Trainer, Motivational Keynote Speaker

Table of Contents

Foreword

Some connections arrive quietly. Others announce themselves like prophecy.

I first met Jeremy McDonald by what I now know was divine choreography. It was 2018, and I was in Mt. Shasta with a friend on a weekend retreat — one of those weekends where the air feels charged with possibility. We were wandering into a small crystal shop when she asked, almost casually, *"Have you ever thought about speaking on a cruise?"*

The image flashed through my mind — a stage at sea, sunlight pouring through wide windows, waves stretching endlessly beyond the deck. I felt it for just a moment, then let it go. Two days later, a message arrived in my inbox inviting me to speak on the **Spirit Heart Cruise.** That was my first lesson in what Jeremy would later call *Divine Timing. Divine Order. Divine Plan. Make it Easy.*

It was on that cruise that I met Jeremy — not just as a fellow speaker or cruise host, but as a kindred soul. There was a night when we sat together in a group and something in both of us simply knew: we were meant to do great things together. At the time, we didn't know what form that would take. We only knew it was vibrational resonance.

From that moment on, our paths wove together — sometimes running parallel, sometimes intersecting, always orbiting the same north star. There were seasons when he was ahead and offered me guidance, and seasons when I walked a few steps before him and reached back to offer a hand. Our lives, our lessons, our missions — all of them seemed to evolve in tandem.

And that is what makes this book so profound. *The Sovereign Mindset* — is lived wisdom, not just a philosophy. It's the hard-won truth of someone who has wrestled with his own patterns, confronted his own programs, and walked through both light and shadow to embody what sovereignty truly means.

The pages ahead speak with the voice of someone who has walked the fire and gathered wisdom from the embers. Each insight is distilled from moments that shaped him, lessons that rewired him, and truths that continue to expand him. The questions woven through these chapters go straight into the places within us that most need awakening. One question in particular stopped me in my tracks:

"Have I made someone else's needs more important than my own in the name of love?"

I paused. I reflected. And I realized how many times I had betrayed myself under the banner of love. That is the power of this book. It *interrupts* you. It holds a mirror to your soul and asks if you're ready to meet yourself there. That is the heartbeat of the Sovereign Mindset.

For years, I watched Jeremy make manifestation look effortless. Opportunities seemed to unfold around him with almost magical ease. I used to wonder what his "secret sauce" was. Now I know: it's a frequency. A state of surrender wrapped in certainty, embodied in one timeless phrase:

Divine Timing. Divine Order. Divine Plan. Make it Easy.

These pages reveal how that state is cultivated by *aligning deeper.* By clearing the "wishy-washy" energy that confuses the universe and replacing it with unwavering clarity. By listening to the whisper within rather than the noise without. By remembering that the law of attraction is not about what we want, but about *who we are.*

As you read, you'll feel this book shift from words to initiation. It will challenge the false stories you've inherited. It will illuminate the subtle ways you give away your power. And it will call you home — to the quiet authority of your own soul.

And perhaps most beautifully, it will remind you of this truth: we attract people who match our frequency. Most of the time, those people come and go — reflections, lessons, mirrors. But every once in a while, the universe sends someone whose evolution intertwines with yours. Someone who doesn't just walk beside you — they grow with you.

Those are the rare friendships. The sacred ones.

The ones that don't just witness your transformation — they *become* part of it. And that is what Jeremy McDonald has been to me. My hope is that, as you step into the pages of this book, he becomes that for you too.

— Dawna Campbell, Founder of The Abundant Soul, International Best-Selling Author, and Executive Vice President, The Los Angeles Tribune.

Introduction

Fellow reader, let me tell you a little bit about myself so you can better understand my journey. I was born to two teenagers in 1974 in Minneapolis, Minnesota. About a year after I was born, my father and his family moved to Phoenix, Arizona. After that, my parents lost touch until I was 11 years old.

Growing up, I often felt different from the other kids at school because I didn't know my father. Over the years, that absence created a quiet resentment within me—a wound that would take time and understanding to heal. Thankfully, my father and I now share a wonderful relationship built on mutual respect.

I was raised by my mother, who was both a nurse and an energetic healer—a shaman in her own right. She passed down her wisdom to me and became my first teacher in the art of healing. Over the past twenty-eight years, I have walked a dual path: one as a learning and development professional, and the other as a metaphysical minister, energetic healer, and coach.

Through both of these paths, I earned my ordination from my mother and a master's degree in Adult Education. For a long time, I believed that my worldly accomplishments and professional accolades defined my worth. But what I've come to understand—and what I hope to share with you through this book—is that while I am proud of what I've achieved, it is *who I have become* through all of life's experiences that fills me with the deepest sense of pride and gratitude.

As I start this book, I want to remind my readers that it is the journey, not the destination that they should focus on. Why? Because we discover things about ourselves in the journey that we would not have known by not taking the necessary steps in our journey. As I have continued down my spiritual path, I have seen and learned many things in my life simply through the act of living, and this suggests that it is everyday living that shapes us into better versions of ourselves. A journey is much like following the yellow brick road—you'll encounter problems, face challenges, and experience success along the way, just as Dorothy did. You will make mistakes, but the most important thing you will do is evolve. So, start getting excited about growing and learning more about who you really are on a higher level.

Another thing you will do while you grow is change, and in the change process, your priorities and reasons for doing things will evolve. This leads me to the reason why I am writing this book. To understand this, I need to explain why I started down my spiritual path.

I started studying different spiritual texts, metaphysics, self-help topics, and psychology in my teen years because human potential was fascinating to me. Then, about 17 years ago, I went through my own "dark night of the soul" – which is a time of spiritual transformation marked by confusion, despair, and inner turmoil. During this time, it was up to me to practice all the information I had studied for so many years. In other words, I had to start putting my knowledge into action.

After losing most of what I thought was important in my life, I had no other choice but to start using the tools I had learned through my studies. So, I started a policy in my own life that I had to try the techniques I was teaching others on myself first; this way, I could practice what I was teaching before I recommended the techniques to others.

Through my process of healing, I discovered hidden layers of my own self-doubt, limiting thoughts, and inner suffering. Like many, I carried beliefs and programs handed to me by others and shaped by how I perceived the world around me. I had a mental image of the world that felt like the world was working against me, and I would feel this pressure in my body that felt heavy, depressing, and reactive to the world around me. I was a prisoner in my own mind, and it was difficult not knowing when I would be released.

At the end of 2011, I wrote a book called *Peace Be Still*, inspired by the part of my journey I had taken up to that point, and it was a well-received book. I continue to get comments from people who this book has helped even today. However, that book was just the beginning of an even longer journey because I would sit down to write another book beyond *Peace Be Still*, and I would get writer's block. I could write posts for social media, articles for magazines, and even for work, but when I sat down to write my next book, my mind would go blank, or I would start to judge what I was writing. Then, the judgment would block any further flow of creativity. Everything I tried to write felt insufficient.

The tricky part of all of this was that I was having profound experiences—one of the most significant being a "shared death" experience. This phenomenon occurs when a living person participates in some aspect of another's dying experience. I encountered this firsthand when my mother passed away.

At the time, I was in the middle of writing *Peace Be Still* when my mother transitioned into spirit. I came to realize that it simply wasn't the right time for me to write that book. I hadn't yet lived through the experiences or gained the wisdom necessary to write from the depth of understanding I now have.

I want to emphasize this because I've been interviewed about my shared death experience and have spoken about some of the extraordinary moments that left me utterly in awe—moments so profound that I could hardly pick my jaw up off the floor. Yet, the truth is that none of these experiences meant anything without the lessons that came from them. We can have the most incredible experiences in life, but unless we use them to grow into better versions of ourselves, we miss the true purpose of life itself: the evolution and awakening of the soul.

One story I will tell you about here started me on a new journey of discovering who I am and who the rest of us are. It was April 2013. I had been home from my book tour for about six months and needed to go back to work, i.e., a regular job, so I started praying for the highest and best job opportunity for me. I knew the universe would take care of me and give me more than I needed. I got an interview for a Training Specialist position and went in for the interview. I remember walking into the office building where the interview was. I saw the marble pillars, the beautiful lobby, and the gold elevator. A thought in my head popped up, saying, "Now entering Prince Jeremy McDonald of the Kingdom of the Universe." I remembered how empowered I felt after hearing this in my mind, but at the same time, I felt at peace, excited, joyful, and just passionate about the interview, which, fortunately, went well. In the interview, the interviewers said how much they enjoyed meeting me, and that they were pretty sure I would hear back from them that day. I returned to my car and prayed again, saying, "That or better. If it's not this opportunity, I know you have something better for me."

I got that job but only worked there for about a month and was given a severance package, which I'm sure you realize is not a very common work practice for such a short tenure. Several months later, I got a letter from the same job, and they gave me an additional check after my severance had been paid out because they realized they had given a raise to that position and wanted to pay me the missing amount I would have made for the time I worked. I had to stop and ask myself how many companies would do this for someone who no longer worked for them?

I tell you this story because of what it taught me and how it showed me who you and I are. We are very simply a child of God. We are made in their image, as stated in Genesis 1:26-27:

> Then God said, "Let us make mankind in our image, in our likeness, so that they may rule over the fish in the sea and the birds in the sky, over the livestock and all the wild animals, and over all the creatures that move along the ground."

I share this story to show how I've learned to reflect on my life and use my experiences for growth. For me the supernatural is just as meaningful as every day, because life gives us exactly what we need to thrive as souls. Our success depends on following the inner guidance that resonates with our deepest truth.

The reality is we all have one mission but many paths to get there. The one mission is to get to know ourselves. On a much more profound basis, we need to have a relationship with that divine spark in each of us. This means we follow that innermost feeling or voice guiding us to happiness and the highest and best good that we can put out in the world. This part is essential for us all to understand because, in our world, we follow opinions, ideas, and journeys, and we hang on to others' words for our guidance, security, and happiness, some of which can be to our detriment as I'm sure you've experienced. As you read this, you may ask why that is the case. The answer is this: follow what you feel. If you hear someone say something that resonates with your soul, then yes, that is an energy that is guiding you to new growth for your soul, but if you hear something that does not resonate with you and your inner world is saying something different, then you go with your inner voice. Your inner world has the final say regarding how you want to live.

No doubt I know some are thinking, well, this is easier said than done, and I agree with you. Some would say, well, if everyone just did what they felt, then there would be no order in the world. This I don't agree with because if we were following our inner guidance, then we would be following the divine order and that in and of itself is the governance we need to guide us in our lives. Understand that the divine order is not separate from you. It is you, and this is part of the issue all of us have. We feel so separated from the source that gives us life, but what we really feel separated from is our souls.

Our world is geared towards worrying about the world around us, being concerned with how others live their lives, and spending time trying to control how we present ourselves to the world, how we are perceived in the world, and how we are accepted in the world. These programs or mantras have been around for thousands of years and have appeared differently throughout those many years, but they have always been there. These same programs make us feel insignificant, make us compare ourselves to others, judge others, and affect us on such a level that it hurts our physical health and stunts our soul's growth. It is now time for all of us to be empowered enough to stand up and live life the way we know will be the highest and best for us and not by what is dictated to us by others.

I will create a dialogue in this book because the process is to pay attention to your inner dialogue, have a relationship with it, love it, listen to it, and, most of all, heal it. Think about these questions and ponder them for just a minute:

1. How often have you thought you should speak up about something and do not because you did not want to rock the boat or deal with the response to you speaking up?

2. How often have you thought about doing something but have yet to do it? (For example, getting healthier, saving money, accomplishing career goals, etc.)

3. How often have you promised yourself that you'll never do something again but then do it anyway?

4. How often have you denied yourself the opportunity to pursue your desires because you didn't think it was possible?

Asking yourself these questions creates a baseline for telling yourself when you have gone against yourself. These moments of going against ourselves prevent us from living in alignment with our souls.

This book is about changing our energy and mindset to be geared toward being at one with our souls. By aligning with our souls, we align with everything else and everyone else.

My mother taught me something her teacher taught her. It was the Mayan term *In Lak'ech*, which means "I am you, and you are me." This tells us that as we cause harm to anyone or anything, we are, in turn, causing harm to ourselves. So, as you do your inner work, you will start to notice that you will treat others better, and the better you treat yourself, you will treat others with the same amount of respect and love.

The last thing I'll say before we get into the chapters of the book is this: this work comes from many years of meditating, processing my life, reading self-help books, and studying texts from many different religions, and on topics such as psychology and emotional intelligence. I have had teachers and mentors, but the greatest teacher I have found is my own inner world. As a result of my journey with my inner world, I have had mystical experiences and personal moments of growth through just living and experiencing life. What I will tell you is that ordinary living moments are just as profound as the mystical moments, and we will explore this throughout the book. This is why I speak about both the mystical and the everyday— because to truly understand the Sovereign Mindset, we must find balance in every area of life. You may be asking, "What exactly is the Sovereign Mindset?" We'll explore this in depth throughout the book, but simply put, the Sovereign Mindset is when an individual takes full authority over their thoughts, actions, and decisions while learning to connect with the higher aspects of themselves in harmony with body, mind, and soul.

Along the way, I'll share some of the teachings and practices I have studied. But more importantly, my hope is that you feel inspired to embark on your own journey—to sit with yourself, to uncover and release the layers of programming that have held you back, and to step fully into your own power.

As you read this book, I challenge you to take time to process what really catches your attention or triggers a thought. Reading this book is not a race; it is meant to inspire an awakening in you and to create your own inner dialogue.

I'll leave you with this thought: throughout this book, I'll be describing the definitions of some of the words I use. Some of you will already be familiar with them because you use them every day, but I include the definitions for those who may not. This book is meant for a wider audience, not just a few. My hope is that it sparks a movement—one where people become more self-aware, more connected to who they truly are, and far more empowered through the pages of this book.

So, let's get into it and have fun with your self-dialogue.

1

Awakening to Your True Self

Many people refer to their "awakening" moment when describing the time in their lives when they entered a new stage of illumination. This could stem from a near-death experience, a dark night of the soul, or any number of profound events. But the truth is, we experience many awakening moments throughout our lives. So, when people ask me, "When was your awakening?" I often reply, "Which one?"

Awakening is a lifelong process. Sometimes the shifts are profound, and sometimes they are subtle. There is no race and no single path to awakening—only the unfolding journey of discovering who you truly are as a soul. This path asks you to peel back the layers of programming, emotions, thoughts, and beliefs that have limited your potential.

Once you begin to realize the vast magnificence of your soul, you'll also realize that most of us have been given a false image of limitation. Our minds operate from a restricted viewpoint, and we misunderstand what true divine potential is. Living with a sovereign mind means knowing who you are and trusting that all things will unfold as needed. Your mind may ask, "But how is that possible? How could I be unlimited?" The answer lies in the inner work. As you explore yourself more deeply, you'll find limiting thoughts, emotions, and energies. The only way to discover your unlimited potential is to transform your inner landscape.

Let's begin with quick exercise. Sit back, take a deep breath in through your nose, and exhale through your mouth. Keep breathing slowly. Close your eyes if you'd like. Now, say to yourself *these words: "Divine Timing. Divine Order. Divine Plan. Make it Easy."*

As you say these words internally, imagine your breath carrying them like a river through your body—releasing tension, stress, and the bondage of old thoughts. Keep breathing and let your inner voice echo these truths through every part of your being.

Now, take another moment. Do you feel peace? Or tension in certain areas? Wherever you are, it's okay. These sensations are your guideposts. On a spiritual or metaphysical level, tension and anxiety signal the presence of stagnant Qi, which in Chinese philosophy is the life force energy that flows through all living beings—often stuck due to trauma from this life, past lives, or even ancestral lineage. Trauma holds us in place until we can find peace with it. Healing doesn't mean forgetting; it means integrating the lessons and reclaiming your power.

I once worked with a client who had suffered severe childhood trauma. Through her healing sessions, she discovered that the trauma wasn't her fault, and as an adult, she had the power to find peace. In doing so, she didn't just free her human self, she expanded her soul.

The human side often lingers in victimhood, but healing begins when we allow ourselves to feel the pain and offer grace to ourselves. Society tells us to "just get over it," but that only represses the wound.

True healing invites grace and releases blame—guiding us gently toward peace.

Healing is never about casting blame. It's about inviting you to see who you are on a deeper level. Whatever you discover within yourself is meant to bring awareness, not shame. You've done the best you could with the awareness you had up until now.

Your path to soul awareness is both beautiful and, at times, difficult. That's because we're dismantling old beliefs. Yes, your physical body is made of flesh and can be harmed—but your soul cannot die. It is eternal, and it is vast—far beyond the comprehension of the human mind.

Through meditation and a shared death experience with my mother, I learned that our souls are constantly in motion—flowing in and out of consciousness. Sometimes tangled, sometimes free. Regardless, the soul always grows. And when we allow ourselves to flow with life instead of resisting it, we evolve.

This comes down to one powerful question: What do you want to serve—*fear or love?*

Your body has an energy field sometimes referred to as the aura, and when you operate from fear, that field shrinks. When you embody love, it expands. This principle is reflected in scripture:

> *"You are the light of the world... Let your light shine before others, so that they may see your good deeds and glorify your Father in heaven."* — **Matthew 5:14–16**

When you serve love authentically, your light grows brighter. And as your frequency rises, people and experiences that no longer align with your energy may fall away. This is natural—everyone should grow in their own direction. Life is always in motion, and the river flows best when you stop paddling against it.

So, why do we resist? Because the world has told us we are broken. We are not enough. We are sinners. You can see the pain of that programming on people's faces—the heaviness they carry in their bodies, their hearts. But the truth is, your outer world reflects your inner world. So, when you have a heavy heart, the world around you will feel and look heavy. When we talk about attracting the life we want, we forget that we attract what we are, not what we desire.

So, if who you are at the deepest subconscious level believes that you are a failure, then that's how the world manifests around you. But if you see yourself as free and at peace, then that's the way the world will manifest around you.

Think of the person (perhaps it's you) who repeats the same relationship patterns: partners who won't commit, who betray, who are emotionally unavailable. These are signs of unresolved inner wounds. If you don't fully love yourself, you'll unconsciously choose people who reinforce that belief. Healing begins when you look in the mirror and see your own worth.

Let's take this further.

Ask yourself—*Why do people never fully commit to me? Then ask— Where have I not been fully committed to myself?*

Maybe you've ignored red flags, withheld your voice, or sacrificed your needs. That's not commitment to self.

Why are they always emotionally unavailable?

Ask yourself— *Where am I not emotionally present with myself?*

Perhaps you've been chasing the future, waiting for someone to change instead of being present and aligned with your own needs.

Why do partners betray me?

Ask yourself—*Where and when have I betrayed myself?*

When you suppress your voice, ignore your truth, or accept less than you deserve, you betray your soul.

Be gentle with yourself as you ask these questions. Offering yourself grace is essential. Beating yourself up only feeds unworthiness. The good news is that the same way the critical voice developed, it can also transform.

There is a loving voice within you. The more you choose that voice, the more the critical voice begins to heal. Instead of condemning, it can become your guide—gently correcting, supporting, and helping you grow. This shift allows you to move through life with more grace, more awareness, and deeper peace.

And that peace? It's sacred. Listening to your inner world is sacred—and so are you. Not sacred in the sense of worship, but because your body is the true temple of God. When you treat your body as sacred space, you naturally honor, love, and care for it—just as you would anything deserving of respect. The difference is that this honor is offered with grace, in harmony with the divine spark within. This is why that deeper peace is so precious, and why you'll feel called to protect it.

The Hidden Programs of the Mind

Like many of you, I have countless stories of success but also examples where I felt I had failed. And like many of you, I spent more time focusing on my failures than I did on the success. What if I were to tell you that both your success and your failures help you attain success in life and that you could not have any type of happiness or fulfillment without having both bad times and good times? All experiences are a blessing because they help us grow as spiritual beings.

One of the most difficult points in my life was in 2006 when I was the vice president of a mortgage company in Baltimore, Maryland. In July of that year, I remember being 32 years old, looking in the mirror in my bathroom, and thinking how miserable I was. When I look back, I see that I was building a story in my mind of success, but I was building a lie about what success was. I thought it was my title, the house I was living in, the boyfriend I had, and the paycheck I was receiving. When I look back at this time in my life, almost 20 years later, I see it so much differently now than I did then.

Taking a hard look at that time, I see a man who was codependent on the people around him. I wasn't in a successful relationship but rather in a toxic one that was damaging for both of us. As I looked at my job and title, I realized I was working for a narcissistic boss who played his managers against each other, messed around with our payroll, caused drama among the employees, and was generally an unpleasant person. Unfortunately, I was too young and naïve to see what was happening around me, so much so that I didn't even see that the roommate I had was also toxic for me.

Now, when I say "toxic," this does not always mean the other person is bad. It means the situation was toxic for both parties. We were young and did not communicate our intentions, frustrations, and problems clearly or authentically. We used passive-aggressive tactics to get the other people to respond in a way that made us feel better. We were toxic for each other. I know we can all relate to this because we've all, at some point in our lives, used passive-aggressive tactics to get people to do what we want and then felt we were successful because they did what we wanted.

The truth is each of us has a divine plan we came into this life to accomplish. When we try to push someone into doing something that goes against their soul, it comes back on us and keeps us from living our own divine plan. This is why understanding who we are on a deeper level—and building a relationship with our inner world—is vital to our success and keep us focused on our own lives and path.

Understanding Our Passive-Aggressive Tactics

A way for us to understand our own passive-aggressive tactics is to ask ourselves the following questions:

- Have I tried to make someone feel guilty about how they made me feel instead of clearly communicating how I feel?

- Have I blamed other people for my low self-esteem instead of taking the time to heal my wounds from the past and effectively come to peace with my past?

- Have I called someone names when I was angry and belittled them for actions or behaviors, they demonstrated instead of clearly expressing my boundaries?

- Have I ignored someone and given them the cold shoulder when they upset me instead of just talking to them about what is bothering me?

- Have I aggressively questioned someone about their actions instead of clearly expressing my own feelings that were a response to their actions?

These are just a few questions we can ask ourselves to see if we are trying to emotionally manipulate someone into behaving the way we want them to instead of just clearly expressing how we feel and setting our boundaries.

The Programming We Receive

The reality that most of us may not be aware of is that we learned our ways of communicating through the adults around us as children. Children mimic the adults around them, whether those interactions are healthy or not, much like how a child learns a language in the first few years of their life. We learn how to socially interact with others based on what we witness and how the people around us respond when we are kids. This same kind of programming is given to us in television, movies, social media and schools.

Now, we are not here to blame the people who were around us when we were kids or adults. We should hopefully be grateful to those who helped shape who we are today, and we also, as adults, get to decide who we are now and not be defined by other people's ideas. When we were growing up, our parents, teachers, and adults around us gave us a foundation; however, it was not meant to give us a strict map of how to live or behave in the future. After all, some of us grew up with a better, sturdier foundation than others. The point being, whatever that foundation or programming we received in our youth, we need to learn from it going forward in life.

Lessons Learned from My Mother

As I have looked back at my life, especially with how I was raised, I remember my mother was a dreamer. She gave me permission to be as creative as I wanted to be and taught me to give it my all whenever I worked on something. That was a solid foundation, but I was also raised in a church that made me fear God. My mother attended that church until I was about 14 years old, when she decided for herself that she could no longer associate with a church that taught people to fear God. She said she could no longer support a church that taught fear over love and could hardly believe that a loving God would do the things that this church taught us. She also gave me permission to stay in the church or leave. She did this because she had taught me to think for myself. She empowered me to make my own choices especially when it came to my own spiritual beliefs. This, in a sense, was one of the greatest gifts she could have ever given me because it allowed me to think for myself and build a foundation that was mine.

The Roots of Not Valuing Myself

So, where did I begin to lose the ability to value and love myself? Like many of us, it started with what I saw and absorbed from the adults around me. I grew up in a church that didn't celebrate birthdays, Christmas, or most of the holidays others looked forward to. By the sixth grade, I was already six feet tall, which made me stand out— and not in a way that felt good. Add dyslexia and attention deficit issues, and I often felt like an outcast.

My mom was just 16, almost 17 when I was born, a single parent still figuring out life while raising me. In many ways, we grew up together. You can probably imagine that self-esteem and acceptance weren't my strongest qualities. Like my mother, I became codependent—someone who sacrifices their own needs to meet the needs of others. In codependent relationships, one person becomes the giver, while the other assumes the role of the taker. And for much of my early life, I only knew how to be the giver.

Asking the Hard Questions

I started to ask myself the hard questions that most of us don't want to ask, and you can do the same thing with yourself. Take a moment to ask yourself:

- Have I made someone else's needs more important than my own in the name of love?

- Have I compromised my boundaries to avoid rocking the boat, hurting someone's feelings, or avoiding judgment?

- Do I know what my boundaries are and how to articulate them to another person in a proactive and clear manner?

- Do I talk to others about my problems with someone else to get them to rally on my side, so I feel better instead of just talking to the person who is hurting me?

- Do I procrastinate on working toward things that bring me joy because I'm so wrapped up in how terrible my life feels right now?

I ask these questions mainly to get you to start thinking, and you may need to ask yourself other questions that relate more closely to your life. The main point of asking these questions is to start processing where you are in your life and build your self-awareness so you can begin making different decisions. My true journey started the day I looked into the mirror as the vice president of that mortgage company and realized how unhappy I was. That moment sparked the journey to where I am today. These are just a few of the many questions I asked myself over the years, but I started with these so I can break down the process of how these questions can bring you increased awareness of yourself.

The First Question: Self-Worth and Love

The first question was: *Have I made someone else's needs more important than my own in the name of love?*

This started with a statement my mother made to me when she was 49 years old, and I was 32. She said to me that she had been a mother, a daughter, a good friend, and a nurse all her years, but she had not really got to know herself and explore the things she wanted to explore for herself. She said to me that she loved me very much, but that she was going to start getting deeper into healing work. She was getting ready to start an apprenticeship in shamanic healing, as well as other modalities because it was what her soul had been calling her to do for a long time.

This realization really hit me when I asked myself whether, in all the hats I wore—friend, boyfriend, son, vice president, and so on— this led me to see that I had never truly made my own life and soul a priority. The honest answer was no. That's when I told myself I was going to write a book and become a motivational speaker. At the time, I had no idea what kind of journey that statement would take me on.

Shortly after, I lost my VP role due to the changing environment in the mortgage industry. That began a six-month process of losing almost everything I had in my life. This loss eventually led me back home to Florida, where I started down a path of self-discovery to answer a simple but profound question: *What truly makes me happy?*

One thing I did know was how much I had enjoyed being a corporate trainer in the past. I loved watching people learn, grow, and succeed. We'll explore this later when we talk about natural law, but one of the greatest truths about teaching is that you receive just as much as you give. There is a natural ebb and flow—you learn as you teach, and in turn, your students teach you as much as you teach them.

Then, I was reminded of a lesson my mother taught me during my Reiki attunements: *'Healer, heal thyself.'* As those words came back to me, I realized that while I was calling myself a healer, speaker, and coach, I wasn't fully practicing what I preached. I had plenty of knowledge, but not a deep, practical understanding of it because I hadn't yet done the inner work of peeling back the layers of illusion I had built around myself.

I would get excited when I helped someone shift something in their life, but I didn't see that, for me, it was only a temporary fix. That was because I hadn't fully learned to be okay with who I was in the moment. One of the biggest healing lessons you will ever have is to accept who you are on all levels. It's one thing to understand something intellectually, but unless you embody and feel the lesson, it can remain a temporary patch over a deeper issue.

I also struggled with insecurity because I was worried that people might find out I still had baggage of my own to work through. The truth, though, is that we all carry baggage—and working through it is part of the lived, human experience.

The Search for Love and Acceptance

Years after I wrote my first book, it occurred to me one day that I had literally been searching for love and acceptance. I sought quick fixes, such as people giving me compliments about how I had helped them with whatever they had been working on. I also took pleasure in doing nice things for my friends and loved ones, but I got more joy out of that than I did from doing nice things for myself. This went on for a long time until I was once again hurt by a group of friends for not telling me the truth about something that had been going on. As much as it hurt, it taught me how I had ignored the red flags and signs that had been shown to me time and time again—not just in this situation, but in many others before it.

When I realized that making them smile made me happier than making myself smile, I knew something was out of balance, and it was time to do something about it.

Then, the epiphany came: there is nothing wrong with helping people be successful, and there is nothing wrong with doing things to make others smile. But it must start with you. You must work on making yourself happy first, and that begins with your own healing. Once you've done this, you can create a healthy balance and boundaries when helping others.

When you heal yourself first, the things you do for others are no longer draining—they are aligned, balanced, and filled with healthy boundaries. They become even more enriching than before because they flow from you being a whole, authentic person who gives from the heart and for the heart.

The Second Question: Compromising Boundaries to Avoid Judgment

The second question: *Have I compromised my boundaries to avoid rocking the boat, hurting someone's feelings, or avoiding judgment?*

I have not met many people who truly enjoy confrontation, and there are those, like me, who *really* do not like confrontation. But here is one thing I have learned—if you are a whole person, you will know how to say something in a way that speaks the truth about how you feel without tearing another person down. If they truly care about you, they will take what you say and really try to understand it and change. The ones who do not understand, do not want to change. If they do not even consider your feelings, then they really don't need to be in your life anymore.

This is a hard pill to swallow for most people because sometimes the person you should let go of is truly significant in your life, such as a child, spouse, parent, or a friend who has been with you for many years. Losing them will feel like losing the one person who gets you, loves you, or, at one point in your life, filled a gap you thought would never be filled. The hard truth, though, is that those gaps or voids need to be filled by you and your relationship with your soul, not by other people.

Cultivating the Divine Within

Recently, I was reminded of Psalm 23, which I had memorized as a child. You may already know the verse, but I encourage you to read it now and really feel it:

> *The Lord is my shepherd; I shall not want. He makes me lie down in green pastures;*

> *He leads me beside the still waters. He restores my soul;*

> *He leads me in the paths of righteousness For His name's sake.*

> *Yea, though I walk through the valley of the shadow of death,*

> *I will fear no evil; For You are with me; Your rod and Your staff, they comfort me.*

> *You prepare a table before me in the presence of my enemies; You anoint my head with oil;*

My cup runs over. Surely goodness and mercy shall follow me all the days of my life;

And I will dwell in the house of the Lord Forever.'

This time, the verse affected me differently because I was paying attention to how it made me *feel.* First, I believe the temple of God is within. When you truly embrace that idea—rather than just reading the words—you begin to understand that God, or the divine, dwells within you.

This scripture reminds us that there is a force guiding and protecting us—but it's not some man with a white flowing beard in the sky. That divine presence lives within us. And then, the last line says: *'I will dwell in the house of the Lord forever.'* Take a moment to feel that. God's house is not somewhere outside of you—it is within you.

When you cultivate that inner relationship with the divine, you realize you are never alone, never lost, and never lacking. But to truly experience this, you must understand it on a deeper level than just the surface of the words.

When you let go of someone because being around them no longer serves that deeper, soulful part of you, you send a message to your inner world about how important it is to you. You are showing that you will no longer compromise who you are for another person. You will never be a prisoner in your life to how others treat you because you felt you needed them in your life to feel loved. I say this very strongly because we shout a lot about freedom in this world, but when we trap ourselves in unhealthy situations for years without ever saying anything, are we truly free? And, if we are not free, who is really holding us hostage?

The Third Question: Understanding and Articulating Boundaries

The third question: *Do I know what my boundaries are and how to articulate them to another person in a proactive and clear manner?*

I realized I didn't even know what a boundary was—or why I would set one—until it became clear that boundaries aren't meant for other people; they're meant for us. For years, I ignored my own boundaries. I let people flake on me, I excused poor behavior as 'patience,' and I stayed silent when others spoke to me in ways that weren't okay. It took time to understand that I did have boundaries—I just wasn't honoring them or communicating with them clearly.

The truth is, we're never really taught about boundaries. There's no class in school that shows us how to set them. Media and television often portray life with no boundaries at all, while still pushing ideas of how we should act to be accepted. Even in the news, we hear about wrongdoings immediately, but the consequences—the boundaries— don't come until much later. In the meantime, the harm continues, unchecked.

I can tell you that expressing your boundaries takes practice, and like all things that require practice, you will not get it perfectly right away. It's important for you to start setting them now. I would suggest that when something upsets you or makes you uncomfortable, you sit for a bit, process the situation, and make clear about what exactly upsets you. Then, approach that person in a calm, confident, and clear manner. Tell them how you felt about the situation and ask for their understanding because a lot of times, they probably did not intend it the way you received it.

When it comes to situations you no longer want to be a part of, such as drinking alcohol or eating too much, you must ask yourself why you continue doing something you no longer want to do. In my case, drinking was affecting my health on a much greater scale than I realized, and I had already been thinking about stopping for a while. I had been getting a clear message about it for some time. So, when my body finally forced the decision on me, I realized I had not been paying attention to the signs, and this was not developing a healthy relationship with myself or my soul.

The Fourth Question: Talking to Others About Problems

The fourth question: *Do I talk to others about my problems with someone else to get them to rally on my side, so I feel better instead of just talking to the person who is hurting me?*

Now, when I bring this question up, I am not talking about when you go talk to a professional coach or therapist who is helping you process a situation. I am speaking about situations when you go to your friends (or anyone who will listen) when you are upset to complain or gossip about another person so that you can get people to agree that you are right and they are wrong. This almost always means that you are not secure in your own understanding of the situation and need validation from other people about your feelings. The reality is, if you go directly to the source, you may better understand someone's intentions, and the only way to find out is to talk directly with that person. This gives you both an opportunity to express yourselves authentically.

Countless times in my life, I have had situations that have hurt me, and I went to my friends to talk about it and never directly to the source. What I saw happening time and time again was that my friends would side with me and then be upset with the person I was talking about. So, what did this do? It turned my friends, even if only for a moment, against that person or persons and energetically, as well as emotionally, started building a potentially false idea about this person. Then, I would go talk to the person and hear their side of the story and realize I was seeing it incorrectly. I then had to apologize and clear the air with the people I had talked to about the situation. Not exactly a mature or productive way to go about life, right?

Finally, I just started going directly to the source and asking for clarity, as opposed to gossiping, and that's what it really is if you really think about it. If I needed to process something, I had one person I would talk to about it who would remain neutral and tell me the truth even if I didn't want to hear it because it would give me a benchmark to work with toward understanding my own place in what was upsetting me. This is something you can tell your friends and loved ones: tell me the truth no matter what because it only helps me become more aware of my blind spots. You do not want a group of people around you who just tell you what you want to hear because then you will build a life of illusion around you that is not authentic.

The Final Question: Procrastination and Joy

The final question: *Do I procrastinate on working toward things that bring me joy because I'm so wrapped up in how terrible my life feels right now?*

This is a deep question because I look back at the many times I procrastinated, and this book is a prime example of this considering how long it took me to work on it and finish it. I finished writing my first book in 2012, republished it in 2017, and now it is 2025, and I am working on the second book. So, 13 years between books is a long time. As I said before, I had to learn before I could finish writing, and one of those big lessons (for me) is procrastination. There was a whole array of thoughts holding me back. I judged the things I was writing, thought about the feedback from the first book—was I good enough to write about these things? Who am I to write about these topics? The list of thoughts and judgments goes on and on. Sound familiar? It wasn't until it occurred to me that all I needed was to my authentic self to write from my heart with my own understanding. Ultimately, who was I writing for? The answer to that question is that I was writing for me, so I could express the thoughts I had daily through my own learning and understanding. And if that evolution helps others, then that was wonderful, but if it doesn't, then I did what I needed to do, and that was being authentically me.

We procrastinate for many reasons, but what I have found in my clients as well as in myself is that we start to get overwhelmed by a task that we need to complete or goals we have set for ourselves because we are too far in the future or in the past but not living in the moment. As a result, we "get into our heads," and this makes us give up on the things we want to work toward.

A common example is weight loss or anything surrounding our health. In my case, weight loss seemed almost hopeless because I would lose weight and gain weight all my life, but what was making me fluctuate? The truth in that was my own thoughts and feelings about myself that were based on the opinions of others. I, like a lot of us, was thinking way too much and not feeling enough. When we feel, we can process our emotions, get to the root of the problem, and start to have peace in our lives.

A lot of my feelings came from childhood and comparing myself to other people. They had higher degrees than me, so they must be smarter than me; they had more money than me, so they must have had opportunities that I don't have. We could go on and on with the list of reasons why I was procrastinating or why any of us do, but what it really comes down to is how we value ourselves, and that value does not fully come until we authentically embrace all of who we are on a soul level. This means accepting all the bad decisions you have made, all the wounds, scrapes, and scars you have, and realizing that all of it makes up who you are right now.

So, ask yourself, why are you procrastinating on whatever it is? What is preventing you from moving forward? I not only ask myself these questions, but I also start doing small tasks so that as I complete those tasks, I create action and momentum forward. I also start paying attention to my thoughts as I take those small steps. This way, I can take the time to become aware of the deeper reasons why I am holding myself back and not proceeding forward.

All the ideas we hold about ourselves shape how we interact with others. That's why it's so important to pause and reflect before we act or speak—so that what we express comes from an authentic place. Speaking authentically simply means expressing yourself from your truest self—in other words, from your soul.

It's equally important to take time each day to get quiet and pay attention to your thoughts and feelings. Time spent on introspection is always well spent.

Before we close this chapter, I want to offer you a simple yet powerful exercise in self-awareness. Our bodies are incredible messengers of truth—often revealing what the mind tries to hide. When something aligns with our soul, our body responds with a sense of lightness and peace; when something is out of alignment, we feel tension, heaviness, or discomfort.

In this exercise I want you to make the following statements to yourself and pay close attention to how your body responds. Do you feel tense or uncomfortable? Or do you feel a sense of ease, happiness, or even a gentle tingling throughout your body as you say these words?

- I am worthy of love and happiness.

- I am worthy of a fulfilled life full of happiness and joy.

- I am worthy of being in relationships where we both mutually value and respect each other for *all* of who we are on an authentic level.

- I am worthy of financial security and abundance.

- I am worthy of a healthy physical body that is full of energy and resilience.

You can add more statements as you see fit, but the key is to feel your body's response. If you feel a tingling all over your body, that is your soul saying "yes!" If you feel anywhere in your body that feels heavy, tense, or anxious, that is a block you want to explore. Ask yourself, "Why is this here? Where did this come from? When did this happen?" and then of course, how can I fix this?

The goal is to develop a deeper relationship with your mind, body, and soul, and allow them to work in harmony with each other, rather than in resistance. Resistance comes from fear, not love. Ask yourself, "Why would I serve fear when I know that serving love for my own inner temple will lead me to what I already deserve as a child of God?" Serving love keeps you in flow with your soul and crowns you with the sovereign mind that is already within you.

3

Embracing Your Soul's Authenticity

It was around 2013, about the same time I had that job interview I had mentioned in the introduction of this book, when I had a dream about standing on a stage in front of a large audience. Let's just say it was roughly about 1,000 people, and I remember it very clearly. I paused for a moment and asked, "Does anyone have any questions or comments?" Immediately, the whole room began talking all at once. Naturally, I couldn't hear or understand anything that was being said; it was just a jumble of noise. Everyone was trying to be heard, and each person felt that what they had to say or ask was the most important thing for me to pay attention to.

Suddenly it became clear to me that these were the many voices in my head at any given time. And it's probably the same for all of you. Let me explain. As I began processing this, I realized these voices represented the many people I've interacted with and their opinions, which had taken up real estate in my mind. Along with these voices were the emotions tied to them, constantly swirling in the background. It was at that moment that I said to them, the fictitious audience in my dream, "Alright, I want to hear all of you and everything you have to say, but I can only do it one at a time—and we have time."

You see, we have allowed other people and other ideas to take up real estate in our minds, and you can see this manifesting in the world today. Everyone is struggling to be heard, and you can hear the fear in their voices and feel it radiate their energy. Social media is full of people trying to be heard, but I would challenge us to look within ourselves and see if we are truly listening to ourselves, specifically to what our soul and our ego are both saying.

As I began to look within and keep my promise to listen, and as I experienced life going forward after that dream, I started to see what I've been talking about in this book. I had made other people's ideas more important in my life than what my soul was telling me. The many voices were not only other people's ideas and opinions, but also the wounded part of me that felt invalidated. This is because every time I listened to someone else instead of to what my soul was trying to tell me, I was hurting that part of myself by essentially ignoring it.

This is much like a person you love dearly. You're excited about something, but as you try to tell them about it, they don't really show any interest. Eventually, you start to lose faith that this person even cares about you. If this goes on long enough, you begin to wonder if you are someone who can be cared for, and then the toxic thoughts start creeping in. Am I lovable? Do I deserve this person? What am I doing wrong that this person I love so much isn't interested in the things that are important to me?

This is what your inner world is saying, and this is what all those voices were struggling to say at that moment in that dream. This is the reason why it was important for me to take the time to listen to each one of those voices because I had to discern what was mine and what was not mine and then work through the forgiveness process so that I could rebuild the relationship with myself and my soul.

In 2021, after practicing meditation for almost 23 years, I achieved a level of stillness I had never experienced before. This was the first time in a very long time that I had not lived with a roommate or had someone living with me. It was also during this time that I developed a deeper love for myself and finally started noticing that soft, soulful voice that had been there all along. I had heard it before, but like all of us, I had doubted its validity because of all the other mind chatter going on in my head—the voices of self-doubt, limitation, and those voices that blocked me from listening to my authentic self.

As part of your daily practice, you need something that allows you to quiet your mind, and I prefer sitting on my couch, just breathing and calming my thoughts. This can also be achieved by going for a walk in a quiet area in nature, working in your garden, or anything that allows you to quiet the mind chatter. Now, before you put the book down and say, "I can't do that, and I've tried," I challenge you to keep trying. Here's why: When you finally achieve that level of stillness, you will be giving yourself the greatest gift you could have ever given yourself.

Something that most people don't realize is that it's part of the process to struggle in the beginning. This happens because, as you start attempting to quiet your mind, your ego and all those voices that have been struggling to be heard, the voices will fight to stay alive and maintain their real estate in your mind. This is all part of the process. This is also the part of your life where you can face yourself and all your pain in a safe place. So, keep trying.

What was significant about this time in 2021 was that I had just moved into a new apartment—my dream apartment. Much like my time in 2013, when I got that job and felt the energy surging through me as I heard, "Now entering Prince Jeremy McDonald," I experienced another moment of clarity and manifestation. I had decided I wanted to move, and I specifically wanted to move into apartments that I had been eyeing for almost a year. I remember sitting at a restaurant every Saturday, looking at the apartments and saying, "That or better."

Realizing that I wanted to move but needed to make more money, I started applying for jobs. For the first time in my career, I had more companies courting me than I had ever experienced before. One job stood out to me, and I truly felt it was the right one, but I continued to go through the other interviews just in case.

I also found out there was a six-month waiting list for the apartment I wanted. So, I went to look at other apartments, and I started packing at home to create momentum for the move. I just knew everything was going to work out, and I was going to get something that would make me truly happy. There was no doubt in my mind. I knew I had to have a change.

Finally, I got the job offer for the company I felt was the right fit, and within one hour after receiving the offer, two other companies I had interviewed with called me to cancel the next set of interviews. The apartment building I had wanted—despite the six-month waiting list—called me and said they had an opening for the exact floor plan I had been hoping for. Within two weeks, I had moved into my new place, started my new job, and for the first time, I was living by myself. I had never been happier. It really made me stop and think, "How did this just happen?" I have several manifestation stories where things just fell into my lap like this, but this and the time in 2013 just really stood out to me.

I spent the next almost two and a half years pondering what really happened to make this move happen so quickly. I'll dive deeper into this later in the book but what's important to know is that I made a decisive move. Without a doubt, I had decided what I wanted and went for it. There was no wishy-washy energy like I had in the past. That wishy-washy energy creates confusion in your energy and results in wishy-washy manifestations. It's like putting one foot on the brake and one foot on the gas in your car. You're not going anywhere.

So, this is where I want to go with this example. Your soul takes you on a journey to bring you closer to home, and your home is your soul—the temple of God within. When you realize that you are connected on a soulful level to all that is, and that you are a child of the great God, and you truly experience that presence, there is nothing that will match that feeling. You will continue to want to be in its presence.

It is important to understand that you are not separate from this presence, it is you, and you are it. So, when this manifestation happened, just like in 2013, it was invoking that inner part of me that is connected to everything.

Now, here's where it gets interesting because this is also where all the dynamics of my life changed. Many of the people in my life changed, and I was laid off from the first company I worked for. I then took on a consulting job, making very good money, only for that contract to end in August 2023.

I had been hearing my inner voice tell me that something big was going to shift soon, and I was getting myself ready for it. Then, I got the call that they were ending my contract in two weeks. What my inner voice now told me was to lay down and rest.

You can imagine my ego jumping up and saying, "REST? What do you mean, rest?!" I immediately went into panic mode, listing all the reasons why I shouldn't stop working. But guess what I did? I rested.

And it's a good thing I did because a little over a month later, my friend called to tell me she had been on a podcast. Like many podcasts, we didn't think it was that big of a deal, and she had even given out her email address for listeners to contact her. What we didn't realize was that we would end up responding to over 16,000 emails in just three months.

So, what did that mean for me? It meant that because I wasn't tied to a day job, I could help her—and that work ended up providing the income I needed to support myself.

I had just lost my job, and now I was knee deep in another job that inspired me to really embrace my spiritual work and declare that it was no longer a hobby, but my new career. We worked 12 to 14-hour days to keep up with everything. During this time, I was about three months away from the end of my lease, and I decided to move out of my apartment, yes, the one I had looked at for so long.

While I was working long hours, I was also preparing to leave for Scotland on a business trip with Spirit World Travel—where I was taking seven people—so I had zero time to move. Yet somehow, people showed up to help, the financial means came in to cover everything, and it all continued to work in my favor. This is what I call divine flow.

The lessons I have learned from these stories are many. Yes, great things can manifest for us, and we are children of a great God. But there is a divine energy that works through all of us—*that* is the divine nature that created these opportunities for me, not my physical brain or body. Yes, I set the intention and ask for the highest and best good, but it's through the relationships I had built by working through all those voices I talked about in the beginning of the chapter that finally helped me create clear manifestations with divine flow.

This is important because if we do not do the inner work, we will not fully understand or embrace our authentic self. As a result, we won't fully understand what is manifesting around us, and we will continue to feel unsatisfied with our lives. Just like the life I had in Baltimore, where I had the title, the boyfriend, and all the things I thought I wanted—but I was not truly happy because I had not fully understood who I was on an authentic level.

This is why you'll see people manifest great wealth and all the material things we think most people, including ourselves want. But without an understanding of the spiritual side, those manifestations often lead to empty situations. That's why I started looking deeper and began asking for abundance, not just wealth. Abundance brings more than what you need, although not always what you want—and that's where the true fulfillment lies.

It is also why we need to continue to ask ourselves the questions pointed out earlier in this book, and we should continue to do our inner work to understand ourselves and take time for ourselves because we will never fully understand true happiness, true love, or true abundance until we have that union of the body, mind, and spirit that happens when you build a healthy relationship with yourself.

One of the first things I ask a new client is, "What do you truly want out of your life?" And I won't let them tell me physical things like money, career, or marriage. I specifically want them to describe how they want to wake up each day and show up in their life. I'm going to ask you the same question here, and I want you to really ponder these:

- How do I want to feel every day when I wake up?

- How do I want to feel each night when I go to bed?

- At the end of my life, how do I want to look back on it? What feeling do I want to have as I review my life?

Oftentimes, people will say to me, "I want to have a loving family or spouse and a career that makes me feel fulfilled at the end of the day." I push them to answer the three questions above because you will never fully understand joy, happiness, fulfillment, or love until you feel those within yourself and about yourself.

When you can find true appreciation for who you are deep within, the world will naturally manifest itself for you without any issues. You will know without a doubt that nothing will break your peace and that the divine always has your back because you are a child of the greatest family in all the known universe. You are divine royalty and knowing this through every part of your being will bring you the things you desire in the outside world—but first, it starts within. It starts with you building your inner foundation on solid rock, not on a house of cards. When you are in this place, then and only then will you be able to align with your highest and best good.

When I decided it was time for me to change and chose to move in 2021, I was telling God that I no longer wanted to live in the situation I was in. I needed a space that would bring me closer to the temple within. Then, everything fell into place. When I was laid off from my job, God was right there, telling me to rest because of what was getting ready to happen.

The next step in my spiritual growth was going beyond my understanding and pushing myself into a full (and true) understanding of who I was on a soulful level. This is where our journey gets beautiful, and you will need to understand that to step into this level and truly embrace your soul's authenticity, you will need to get quiet—and that takes practice.

After moving out of my apartment at the end of 2023 and returning from my trip to Scotland, I moved in with some friends. I was on a high, and financially, my life seemed to be in order. But then, at the beginning of 2024, everything stopped. At the time, I was upset. I felt betrayed by God and questioned why this was happening when I felt I had been on the right track. Then, one night, as I was lying in bed meditating, a force within me picked me up out of bed, lifted my arms, and said, with a booming voice inside of me, "Think bigger," and then gently laid me back down in bed.

Lying there in awe of what had just happened, I was blown away by the presence I had felt, and I knew it was the God within. I had experienced something similar when I did energy work with clients, where I would feel something take over my arms, but nothing to this level of awareness and experience. I kept wondering what "think bigger" meant but I couldn't get an understanding other than knowing it was something beyond what I was doing—and that meant that I needed to get even more quiet.

However, I was wrapped up in my daily life—worrying about paying bills and rushing to get things done so I could make money to pay those bills. In doing so, I was living the direct opposite of what I had been teaching for so many years. Humbled by what was happening on all levels, I knew I was on the right path, but I couldn't grasp what was fully unfolding until one day, I had a shift. It came to me—a concept I knew on an intellectual level but this time, when it popped into my mind, I felt its clarity and need for expansion. The realization was this: the mind is not in the body. The brain is in the body, but your soul is so vast and so connected on a greater level that it is beyond your brain's ability to comprehend, and it's honestly beyond words.

This means you have access to all parts of yourself both spiritually and physically. Yet, we have been taught to look outside of ourselves to find our happiness. The real, hard truth is that you will never fully understand happiness, love, joy, contentment, or any other emotion that we often believe comes from the outside until you fully embrace it within yourself.

This means embracing every aspect of yourself—not only the parts that bring joy, but also the parts that bring stress. All of it is you, and all of it must be embraced and loved. The whole 'love and light' mindset can be toxic because if we're not careful, we end up ignoring the parts of ourselves that are angry, upset, or sad.

We all must walk through our own dark night of the soul. It is through these experiences that our eyes are opened. Only then can we truly understand the lower aspects of ourselves as deeply as the higher ones—for it's by journeying through the full spectrum of our human experience that we awaken to our wholeness.

Admittedly, when I look back, I have been in some situations where, now that I am older and hopefully wiser, I think, "What was I thinking?" The answer to that question is simple: *I wasn't thinking.* I was in the middle of my addictions, impulses, and generally stuck in a reactive mindset instead of being in balance with all parts of me. I didn't see that I was putting on masks and presenting a great face but not being fully authentic to the world or myself.

This realization can only come through experience, and that experience means going through the high points and low points of our lives so that we can contrast the two worlds. Ultimately, you must decide who you serve. Do you only serve one part of yourself, or do you serve the wholeness of who you are? When you fully embrace all aspects of yourself and serve the body, mind, and soul in synergy, that's when true transformation begins.

Two Bible verses I want to bring up here are the following:

"No one can serve two masters. Either you will hate the one and love the other, or you will be devoted to the one and despise the other."—Matthew 6:24

As we serve the material world and allow other people's ideas of how we should be, how we should act, their ideas of what a sin is, how to build our business, or how we should look, we are serving their ideas and opinions. If what they say resonates with your soul, that is one thing because it means their ideas and your ideas align. However, when your inner world (soul) is saying one thing and another person's idea conflicts with what your inner world is saying, then you are serving their idea and not your soul's.

This is why this next Bible scripture is just as important:

"Stop trusting in mere humans, who have but a breath in their nostrils. Why hold them in esteem?"—Isaiah 2:22

This again comes down to whether you feel it and if it works for you and your soul. If it does, then your ideals match. But if it doesn't, then you put more faith in God and your soul than you would in what another human being is telling you. Just like us, humans are growing spiritually. This means they can lead you astray from your own divine plan, and it also means you are following what is being told to you outside of your inner world instead of what is going on inside of you.

Ask yourself the following:

- Do you look in the mirror and criticize how you look, or do you thank your body for the blessings of how it has served you and carried you in life up to this point, seeing the beautiful creation that you are?

- Do you compare yourself to others, wishing that you had the life they have instead of having gratitude for what you do have right now?

- Do you look at your friends, family, and loved ones with envy over their success instead of blessing and celebrating their success?

- When someone is confident and carries themselves with strength and grace, do you get uncomfortable around them instead of observing and learning from them?

- Do you think more about what is going on in your life and around the world rather than counting the blessings you have right now?

- Do you feel judged when someone points out a blind spot to you or are you grateful for someone telling you about something that can help you grow?

- Do you feel attacked when someone is not polite to you or doesn't treat you well or do you speak up for yourself in a truthful but calm manner?

These are just a few questions to ask yourself because any time you are critical of yourself or others, you are spending more time paying attention to the outside world and not facing what is going on inside of you. Where are your emotions? Who told you to feel the way you do? Where did you get this feeling about yourself? Once you find that answer, and it comes from anywhere other than you, then you are serving the wrong master. This is where you start, and then you begin the work of changing what is going on inside of you and making the decision to serve your inner world and not other people's ideas.

The Law of Attraction: A Universal Truth

Over the last 25 years, there has been so much talk about the Law of Attraction that it has now become a big part of mainstream popular culture ever since the book about it was published. We've been told that positive thoughts create the world around us, and if we keep our words and thoughts positive, we will manifest the world we desire. But I can tell you, from my own experience, that this is the furthest thing from the truth.

This movement has given rise to a new version of toxic positivity that is plaguing the world, preventing us from facing who we are on a deeper physical and spiritual level. It has also contributed to the "love and light" movement, which has people policing the words we say, judging what others are doing, and avoiding the pain within ourselves. It's time for us to go deeper.

This does not mean, however, that we do not create the world around us. We are most certainly part of creating our reality, and our thoughts do play a role, but it has more to do with how we feel about ourselves inside. This is why the title of this book is *The Sovereign Mindset.*

Much like stories of royalty, when they say something, people listened. But in this case, you are talking about your divine, royal self, the soulful part of you that is in charge. When we work in balance with who we are and in harmony with everything around us, we will see the world transform itself in profound ways.

So, what does this mean? It means we attract the world around us based on who we are. If you think you are not worthy of love, then you will attract a world around you that proves to you that you are not worthy. If you think you can't do something, then you are right because the world around you will prove that you are correct.

This is why we should take time to really understand who we are on a deeper, soulful level and follow the process of uncovering who we are at that level. As we've already discussed, the most vital part of your life is building a better relationship with your inner world. Some days this will feel wonderful, and there will be other days when life doesn't feel good at all, and this is simply because you are peeling back layers of your ideas (good or bad) and internal programming (good or bad) that impact on our life one way or another.

On your journey, you will go through your dark night of the soul because this is something everyone who has achieved a deeper understanding of who they are has gone through. Inanna, the ancient Sumerian Goddess, did this with her journey into the underworld, Buddha did this by sitting under the Bodhi tree. And Jesus did this by wandering in the wilderness for 40 days and 40 nights. These stories are not a new concept, and we all understand that we, at times, may have to walk through hard times to finally discover who we are and become even more self-aware.

I recommend declaring to your soul that you welcome whatever it is you need to look at so you can face it, heal it, and come to peace with it. You can also set the intention that you want it to come in the highest and best way possible and to make it easy for you. I'm sure you can admit that none of us want the cosmic two-by-four in our lives. Let's get the lesson that will help us move forward and do what we need to clear it out of the way if it is not helpful.

The Law of Attraction is exactly what it says in the title: we are constantly creating and attracting. What some do not realize is that we are attracting and creating all the time. It's not just when you want a raise at work or want new love in your life. Every minute of every day, you are attracting and creating the world around you. This is done simply by how you see and feel the world around you and how it makes you feel inside.

The good news is you can change this, and even though it is a process, it is something you can start at this very moment. Ask yourself the following and give an honest answer to these questions:

- **Do I feel the world is working against me and that I have no ability to change my circumstances?**

    o   Try changing this thought too: *The world is working in my favor and showing me my blind spots through challenges so that I can improve who I am as a divine being.*

- **Do I feel that I won't measure up to the dreams I have, and therefore, I should not even try, or I give up easily?**

    o   Instead, change this by focusing on your dreams and working toward them one day at a time, one moment at a time. Allow yourself to be adaptable to challenges and grow from each one of them.

- **Have I started many things and never finished them?**

○ Ask yourself: *Am I so afraid of failure that I give up avoiding disappointment?*

- **Am I too old, poor, or out of shape to make a difference at this stage in my life?" try shifting the question to:**

  ○ **What small steps can I take right now that will make an impact on my longevity and quality of life?"**

    ▪ I bring this up because I had a friend with significant health challenges, and one simple thing she did was stretch her legs while sitting in her chair watching TV. Over time, those small movements made a huge impact on her mobility and improved her overall quality of life.

  ○ **For finances, ask: *"What small amount can I set aside on a regular basis that could shift my financial outlook?"*** I say this because there was a time in my life when I just put quarters in a jar. Eventually, it added up to $500—and that small habit sparked a new mindset about saving.

  ○ **And when it comes to age, ask yourself: *"What moments can I enjoy today that will enrich my life right now?"*** This could be times with your children, grandchildren or loved ones. Enjoying a good book or just having coffee and time to reflect on what is good in your life. This is the time for you!

Asking yourself hard questions helps you start to look deeper at what is going on in your life, and it is the first step toward healing. Once you become aware of what is happening, you can begin to look even deeper to identify the programs that are running against your soul's path.

An exercise you can do every day is to stand in front of the mirror, look directly into your eyes, and tell yourself the following statements while taking a deep breath in through your nose and exhaling out through your mouth. It's important to pay attention to what's going on in your thoughts and your body as you make these statements to yourself:

- I am lovable and worthy of being loved.

- I am valuable and worthy of being valued in my life.

- I am worthy of being respected by myself and others.

- I am worthy of receiving love from myself and others.

- I am worthy of feeling fulfilled in my life every moment of every day.

- I am worthy of feeling a sense of belonging surrounded by people who love and accept each other.

- I am worthy of abundance in my life where all my needs are more than taken care of.

These are not just meant to be affirmations because simply stating an affirmation while an old program is still running in the background will result in the old programs working against the new ones. It's important to really pay attention to what your thoughts are saying when doing this exercise.

Are your thoughts racing? Do you feel silly as you talk to yourself in the mirror? Does your eye twitch or are you feeling uncomfortable? These are all natural responses to what you are doing in this exercise. This is because, like many of us, you have been giving love, respect, and other things to everyone else but we have forgotten how to receive it for ourselves.

This also applies to our prayers. If you have trouble receiving from people who are trying to help you or give you a compliment, then you are blocking your supply of abundance on an energetic level. This will be the same when God blesses you with abundance. If you have trouble receiving, you will have trouble receiving on the many different levels of your life.

Maybe when you say the statement about being lovable and worthy of love, old hurts from romantic relationships or memories of being bullied as a kid pop up. These are the voices of pain in your life that you will want to pay attention to and work on healing. You can face that pain and talk to it much like you would if you saw a hurt or scared child—you would give it love so the child knows that he or she is safe and cared for.

As I personally started digging in and facing the things that came up during this exercise, I would have things surface. One example of this was an old relationship. When it fell apart, I felt dumb because I believed I should have known better. I started blaming myself for what happened, thinking I could have done something better to preserve the relationship. I carried that energy of feeling dumb into my next relationship. I would operate in those new relationships carefully, not wanting to rock the boat or hurt anyone's feelings. I gave my all, giving a lot of myself (i.e., presents), but I also didn't express my deepest feelings because I didn't want to be vulnerable. All this was because I was still holding onto the pain from that one relationship that didn't work out.

This made me start to look at where I was at in those moments with that old relationship, seeing the red flags that I could have addressed with my partner at the time in a calm but truthful manner. The reality was that we probably shouldn't have kept the relationship going because it was a long-distance relationship that we tried to make work for over six years. I never considered that it hurt him just as much as it hurt me. We were both young, and no matter what he or I tried, it wasn't going to work because of the physical distance between us. However, that said, it was probably more than just the physical distance between us.

There were other opportunities throughout the years when we were trying to make our relationship work but I would never let anyone be close to me because I was determined to make this long-distance relationship work. When it didn't work out, I blamed him. And even though there were things he could have done better, there were also things I could have done better. As they say, it always takes two to tango.

When I really started peeling back the layers, I also understood that I kept this situation going because it kept me in a relationship with someone that I could call a boyfriend but I didn't have to be fully intimate with him because of the distance. We may have seen each other, but not on the level we would have if we had been living closer to each other. This was a form of not receiving love at the level of intimacy that I could have had if I had given another person an opportunity to get close to me that didn't live as far away.

Then, I started looking at my previous relationships, and what I saw was that every time I would go out on a date with someone I was attracted to, I would get nervous or uneasy. One date stood out in my mind. I was 21 years old, and he was 20. He had blonde hair, blue eyes, and he was kind, gentle, and made me laugh. We went to dinner and saw a movie. I really enjoyed the date, but I never called him again after that because I made all kinds of excuses about why it wouldn't work out.

This made me stop and think. This is not about blaming or shaming myself; it's about becoming aware of a pattern. The situations may not have been the same but they certainly shared a theme of avoiding true intimacy. Naturally, I had to look up the definition of intimacy in the American Psychological Association, and here's what it says:

> *"Intimacy is defined as an interpersonal state of extreme emotional closeness, allowing personal space to be entered without discomfort. It characterizes close, affectionate relationships and requires a deep understanding of each other. Additionally, intimacy involves the consensual sharing of deeply personal information."*

This stemmed back to many situations in my life, starting with my parents being so young when I was born, to the fact that my mother and I moved around a lot when I was a kid so she could find work. I never had a solid foundation of roots until we moved to Florida. Because of this, I had a hard time creating that long-term connection with someone on a deeper, intimate level unless it was with a close friend—and even then, it was only surface-level intimacy.

This didn't start to change until I really began to look at myself and the reasons behind my actions. The fear here was the fear of loss or a feeling of abandonment. So, if I didn't allow myself to get close to someone on that level, so subconsciously, I was keeping myself from feeling that sense of abandonment.

This took me back to my childhood and the situations in my life at that time that made me feel like I wasn't loved or valued. I would talk to myself at that age and tell myself that I was loved, and that I was no longer that young person. I was an adult, and I no longer had to operate from that level of fear. I could be safe and no longer feel abandoned or unloved. I didn't need to do nice things for people just to get them to love me. I could also honor and love myself and allow myself to have my own boundaries.

Before I started doing this kind of healing work, I would walk into the same types of relationships, whether they were romantic or just friendships. I would constantly end up feeling left out, abandoned, or have a sense that people would betray me. When I started to look at the relationships I was getting into and the people I was interacting with or attracted to, I realized I was finding people with similar patterns to mine.

Just like the principle of *likes attract like,* I was walking into these relationships with similar energy—subconscious fears of being betrayed, abandoned, or unloved. I started to date men younger than me because I had a need to feel wanted and needed. But guess what? Most of them did the same things that the previous ones did, feeding my "unlovable" viewpoint of myself.

As you can see, it was a vicious cycle, with all of us picking each other to feed whatever story is going on in our heads. We're feeding those voices in our hearts and with minds that are constantly chattering, no one is ever getting quiet enough to listen to and catch the pattern of self-sabotage. This cycle will repeat itself over and over until we finally realize we are worthy of being in mutually respectful relationships, where we can be safely vulnerable and openly communicate with each other in a healthy way.

Think about this for a moment: a healthy relationship means you can be vulnerable enough to talk about your pain in a way that allows both parties to grow. If a person does not receive your vulnerability, then they are not the right person for you. Relationships require work, and if both parties are willing to put in the effort, then they can blossom and be successful. But if they are not, it will become toxic and harmful to both people.

As you can see, I was manifesting my relationships and attracting exactly what I was feeling about myself—unworthy, unlovable, and not good enough to have the love I truly wanted in my heart and soul. The universe kept saying, *"You are right,"* and I kept choosing individuals who would fulfill how I felt about myself. And they kept choosing me to fulfill how they felt about themselves.

Again, this is not about blame or shame. It's about recognizing the pattern so you can transmute or change the energy within you. I did not love myself and continued to make decisions that went against what I really wanted. The idea is to wake up to who you are—a worthy member of the largest and most glorious family in all of existence.

You are the most beautiful and precious being in your life, and it's time to recognize that in you. As you start to transmute your thoughts about yourself, the energy around you will begin to change. Your manifestations will seem like they are coming in faster because you are no longer wanting one thing but making decisions that align with the other part of yourself that aren't in alignment.

I also remembered that in 2006, I had lost my job and applied for one after another, but I kept getting the call saying they went with someone else. This continued to feed the story in my head that maybe I wasn't that good at my job, and that I should start applying for jobs that better suited my qualifications, jobs where I wouldn't have to feel "not good enough."

This continued until I was in a job interview for a position I really wanted and was qualified for but in the back of my mind, I could hear very faintly, *"No! Freedom!"* At first, I thought, *"What is this all about? Freedom from what?"* When I really started thinking about it, I realized I was equating a job with not having freedom. I used to jokingly call a J.O.B. (Just Over Broke). In this case, the energy behind having a job felt like I was in prison, or that life was being drained out of me and that I would continually be broke.

So, what did I do? I applied for jobs that were easy to get and that took very little effort. This in and of itself had blessings because I was able to work on myself without a ton of stress. But then, one day, a woman I knew said to me, *"With your skillset, why are you in the job you're in?"* She asked, *"Why are you hiding?"* I was hiding because I was tired of being rejected—working in a call center, taking phone calls instead of working in my career as a Learning and Development professional. What was I really hiding from? Me! Avoiding the real theme going on in my head of self-loathing.

However, I will say that this journey was still perfect because I was also building myself back up from all the pain I had been sorting through since 2006. This is where we need to understand that all things happen with divine timing and in divine order. I was supposed to be at those jobs so I could finally hear her words and then take action to build myself back to where I was before ... but this time, with an even more solid foundation built on truth and a deeper understanding of who I was on an authentic level.

These stories I just shared show you the constant dialogue that goes on in our heads and how we will continue to attract similar situations over and over until we break the pattern. This is why getting to know you and building a relationship with your soul will help you break the pattern. As you allow your inner voice to lovingly guide you through your blocks, you will start to see a major change in your life.

CHAPTER 5

Natural Law: Aligning with Universal Principles

I had a teacher who introduced me to the concept of natural law about 25 years ago, and a few years after that, the Law of Attraction started becoming more widely discussed in mainstream society. She once again emphasized that without understanding Natural Law, we would become confused about how the Law of Attraction works. To be honest, by that time, I had already been studying Quantum Physics and Natural Law and was now caught up in the Law of Attraction trend just like everyone else. I would say, "checks in the mail," and sure enough, I'd start receiving checks. I specifically remember a time when I said, "checks in the mail" followed by "$3,000," and within a week, I received two unexpected checks in the mail for $3,000 each. One was for an old account from when I worked at a grocery store at 18 that I had forgotten about, and the other was for a settlement my mother was owed after she passed away. So, you can imagine how excited I was about my manifestation skills. I truly thought I was on top of the world.

At this point, you might be thinking, "Well, that's a good thing, right?" And yes, it was good at the time, but what I was really trying to understand was how this worked. I wanted to figure out why sometimes what I manifested worked well, and other times, it didn't work as well.

In this conversation about developing a sovereign mindset, we aim to work in harmony with our body, mind, and spirit (soul). That said, a sovereign who simply barks orders at the universe without understanding how things work will find themselves stuck, not knowing why they are there. An example of this is someone who builds a successful business and makes tons of money. Sure, they may have all the money in the world, and through Law of Attraction principles, they've set intentions and taken action. But they haven't considered their highest and best good, which leads them into a situation where they have no time for their loved ones, their health, or other things that truly matter. This is why understanding how Natural Law works is vitally important.

One of the main points of Natural Law is that everything vibrates—everything has a musical tone or frequency, including your own body. This is where we begin to understand attraction because we are drawn to each other's frequency. This is also why, when you focus on a thought or feeling, that frequency draws similar energy to you. Therefore, it's important to tune yourself to the frequency you want to attract. You can do this through shadow work, surrounding yourself with people who uplift you and align with others who share a similar path because when you do, you'll lift each other up through your own frequencies.

When we are constantly around people who are not uplifting us or do not match our energy, it can hinder both our spiritual development and theirs. This explains some of the stories I've shared about my own life, where I kept attracting the same types of people—individuals who matched my frequency. In my last relationship, both of us avoided confrontation, which meant neither of us was fully transparent with our thoughts. I would make jokes to try to convey how I felt, and he would either avoid saying what he truly wanted or make elusive comments, with both of us thinking the other should just understand. But when you really look at it, we weren't being honest with each other or, more importantly, with ourselves.

Until we learn these lessons, like being honest, not only with ourselves but with others—we will continue repeating the same patterns and attracting people who match our energy. Consciously, we may ask, "Why does this keep happening to me?" but on a subconscious level, it's because we aren't seeing the deeper lesson. This is why we ask for guidance in our meditation and prayers, seeking our higher self to guide us through whatever we are trying to navigate. As we raise our frequency, both people and circumstances in our lives will begin to change—and most importantly, we will begin to change.

The next law I want to explain pertains to relativity, which simply means that nothing is defined in isolation—it only takes meaning when compared or related to something else. A clear example of this can be seen with the concept of wealth. The definition of a wealthy person can be subjective, as different people have different interpretations of wealth. For some, wealth might mean having billions of dollars, multiple properties, a private jet, and an array of luxury cars. However, for others, wealth could mean living a life of security, confidence, love, and peace. In this case, the concept of wealth is entirely relative, as they say.

Relativity also applies to our understanding of value, quality, and morality, as what one person considers valuable may differ from another's perspective. This variation stems from how everyone relates to the world around them. For example, a financially poor man may aspire to change his circumstances, but he may not yet have a clear sense of what it feels like to be wealthy. This is why it's helpful and recommended to surround yourself with people who have already reached where you want to be or are on a similar path. By supporting each other, you can learn the necessary steps to achieve your goals.

We should all be familiar with the Law of Cause and Effect, which states that for every action, there is an equal and opposite reaction. This ties into what I discussed earlier in the book. If we feel worthless, that is the cause, and the effect will be a world around us that reinforces that belief. However, if we embrace the idea that we are divine royalty, deserving of the highest and best good—blessings of happiness, fulfillment, peace, and a life filled with love—then that is what the effect will be.

I've had many clients who felt that the world was working against them, and as a result, their world constantly felt like a burden—filled with stress and unhappiness. One way to shift this mindset and change the cause, so your effect will be different, is to start counting your wins—or what some might call blessings. You wake up in the morning, that's a win! You get a shower and prepare for a new day, that's a win! When you start celebrating these small victories all day long, it becomes your cause. The effect? A world that feels like one big celebration. Changing yourself starts with the small things, and they build up into big things. This happens because you're actively working on changing your inner world and the world in turn, notices.

This leads me to another law—the Law of Gestation, which basically states that everything takes time to manifest. You set the intention, act, and work toward that intention. It takes time for it to come to life due to many different factors. For example, imagine you needed surgery, and someone approaches you in the hospital, introducing themselves as the person who will perform it. You'd say, "Nice to meet you, Doctor," only to hear them say, "Oh, I'm not a doctor yet; I still have to go to medical school." Are you going to let them do your surgery? I hope the answer is a resounding NO! Even with the best intentions, they aren't ready to perform the surgery because they haven't yet prepared themselves with the necessary education.

This is no different from when you're working toward something in your life—like the financially poor man we talked about earlier. He isn't wealthy due to many factors or circumstance, such as his upbringing, his job, and the list goes on. But the true reason is that he isn't yet a vibrational match for wealth. Imagine if 10 million dollars were handed to him. There's a good chance he'd spend the money quickly because even though the money is in his bank account, he's still operating at the frequency of a poor man. The path to wealth involves not just accumulating the money, but also the mindfulness to handle it, the boundaries to set, and the growth that occurs until one day, something clicks—and it matches the frequency of wealth he set the intention for but he would have to put in the work to finally see his intention come to fruition.

So, gestation not only prepares you emotionally, but also physically, and most definitely spiritually. There is more to it than just setting the intention; there is a journey with the intention. It's a process of growth, of aligning yourself with the life you desire, and preparing to handle it in a way that sustains you. The work doesn't stop once you set the goal—it deepens with each step you take along the way.

Then, there is polarity, which means that everything has an opposite. At its most basic level, this includes up and down, light and dark, good and bad. These opposites can divide us as individuals and separate us from others. This division splits our minds and energy apart because we have not fully understood polarity. We truly are all aspects of ourselves, including the polarity within us. There is a higher and lower part of ourselves, and there is a light and dark part of us. Depending on the circumstances, we can embody both good and evil.

This is why I find the Bible Chapter Matthew 7 so powerful. In verses 1 and 2, Jesus teaches:

> "Do not judge, or you too will be judged. For in the same way you judge others, you will be judged, and with the measure you use, it will be measured to you."

These verses highlight the importance of embracing the full spectrum of who we are, acknowledging both the light and dark, and understanding that judgment only perpetuates division—both within ourselves and with others. Jesus goes on to say in verses 13 and 14:

> "Enter through the narrow gate. For wide is the gate and broad is the road that leads to destruction, and many enter through it. But small is the gate and narrow the road that leads to life, and only a few find it."

What he is saying here is that when you follow your inner voice and refrain from getting caught up in the latest trends or distracted by the outside world—whether through worry, judgment, or internal conflict—you become one with all that you are. By trusting in this inner guidance, and as he mentions in verses 7 and 8:

> "Ask and it will be given to you; seek and you will find; knock and the door will be opened to you. For everyone who asks receives; the one who seeks finds, and to the one who knocks, the door will be opened."

We often spend too much time focusing on external thoughts and energy—dwelling on the past or worrying about the future. When we do this, our energy becomes divided, and because our energy is split, we can't manifest as powerfully as we could if we were fully aligned with our inner world.

A few years ago, I had a conversation with a friend while we were in Hot Springs, North Caroliina speaking at a healer's gathering. We were discussing this very subject and finally realized that the narrow path Jesus describes is the fine line between the yin and the yang. When we are aligned with our souls and connected to our inner world, we move with the outside world in harmony. As we "dance" with the divine, we intuitively know where to be, what to say, and what to do, and when to do it. But when we are out of alignment and paying too much attention to the distractions of the outside world, we become confused, frustrated, and lost.

So, the true path to understanding Natural Law and the Law of Polarity is to nurture our inner world and to strengthen our relationship with our souls.

The Law of Rhythm is the next natural law, and it states that the world works in an ebb and flow, meaning there will always be ups and downs—good times and bad times. Essentially, this is where the phrase "this too shall pass" comes into play. Knowing this truth helps you realize that no matter how difficult the moment you're facing may be, you understand that eventually, things will begin to rise again.

Here's an even more empowering perspective: each time there's an up and down, you grow stronger. I know this because I've experienced losing most of my worldly possessions, losing my job, and being financially devastated by the world's standards twice. The first time it happened, I fell apart and endured a four-year depression. However, the second time it occurred, I kept pushing forward and eventually built my life back up. I was aware of the lessons from the first experience and practiced what I had learned over the years. As a result, the second time I faced such a challenge, it wasn't nearly as hard because of how I showed up to the situation. The second time I knew I was on the right path and that there was a higher purpose happening to me that I may not fully know right then, but that in the end, this too shall pass, and I would be in a much better place.

This law teaches us that every high and low is an opportunity to learn, grow, and prepare for the future. The more we embrace this rhythm, the easier it becomes to navigate life's cycles. When challenging times arise, I've started to speak to my inner world, and what I say is, 'I know you've got me.' This is my way of telling God that I trust I will be taken care of. And in the end, despite the challenges, I was indeed taken care of. All my needs were met, and everything I needed to accomplish unfolded in divine timing and order. It was a valuable lesson (for me) in trusting the divine plan.

The last of the seven natural laws is the Law of Transmutation, which states that energy moves in and out of physical form. Since energy never dies or disappears, we cannot eliminate it, but we can transmute it into a form that better aligns with where we are headed. This is why people often speak of awakening moments or being "born again."

The true born-again experience occurs when you understand and apply the natural laws. By turning inward and practicing these principles, you begin to transmute the energy within you. Through the Law of Gestation, you transform both spiritually and physically, allowing yourself to be "born" into a newer version of who you are.

This journey mirrors the 22 cards of the Major Arcana in the tarot deck. It begins with the Fool card, which symbolizes new beginnings, innocence, boundless potential, and the excitement of stepping into the unknown. At this stage, you're filled with enthusiasm for the future, even if you're unsure where the path will take you. As you progress through the stages of life, you eventually reach the final card—the World, which represents wholeness, achievement, fulfillment, and completion. It signifies coming full circle and being ready to begin a new phase of growth.

This cyclical journey is what ultimately brings you into alignment with your sovereign mind.

The key takeaway is that no one can override natural laws, and they cannot be bypassed. Understanding the laws of the universe helps you navigate them and foster a better relationship with your sovereign mind. When we resist the natural order, we often find ourselves living a life full of stress, disappointment, and heartbreak. However, this is practice, and through this practice, we grow, learn, and evolve.

This is something you can change right now. When you face challenges, instead of thinking the world is working against you, start embracing the challenges as opportunities for growth. Every challenge you encounter is a chance to align more deeply with your true self and your soul's journey. Let's begin by reflecting on the following questions:

- *When you don't have enough money for something, how do you handle it emotionally?*
- *Do you stress out and feel like a failure?*
- *Do you worry about how you'll get by? Do you blame yourself for past spending decisions?*

Rather than falling into these emotional patterns, ask yourself:

- *Were there any opportunities for me to be more balanced with my finances?*
- *What could I have done differently that I can learn from and apply in the future?*

Remember, this isn't about shame or blame; it's about processing the lesson, learning from it, and integrating those lessons into practice.

Once you've processed the lesson, shift your focus to your energy. Ask yourself:

- *How do you view money?*
- *Do you believe it's the root of all evil?*
- *Do you hold onto the belief that 'money doesn't grow on trees'?*

Instead of clinging to these limiting beliefs, change your perspective to something more empowering. Take heart this affirmation: "I will always have more than enough for my needs, and as a result, I live an abundant life filled with joy, fulfillment, and opportunity."

By shifting your perspective and energy toward abundance, you can align with a healthier, more prosperous mindset.

Here is an additional but important question to reflect on:

Is my health something that just happens to me, or do I have the power to change it?

While it's true that in the physical world, there are factors beyond our control, and many circumstances unfold due to a combination of your soul's mission, in the environment around you, and even with the food you eat, there's still a lot we can influence in terms of our physical health.

Let's take weight loss and changing health dynamics as an example. In my own experience, I was about 60 pounds overweight. Much of this stemmed from low self-esteem, a lack of boundaries, and other factors that influenced the direction of my health. A significant turning point occurred in June 2024, when I was hospitalized for 24 hours after experiencing sharp chest pain and extreme fatigue. Given my family history, the emergency room doctor suspected a potential heart attack, so I was admitted for observation and testing.

At the end of it all, I was diagnosed with type 2 diabetes, obesity, and hypertension—thankfully, no heart attack. This moment was a turning point for me. While many aspects of health are influenced by genetics and the environment, we also have the power to take charge of our health. It's not always easy, but through conscious choices and the inner work we do, we can improve our physical, emotional, and spiritual well-being.

From a metaphysical perspective, diabetes is often linked to sustained anger. I had been carrying anger for years—from childhood experiences, feelings of abandonment, failed relationships, and a sense of inadequacy about where I thought I should be in life. I was pushing myself too hard, managing stress through drinking, and distracting myself with social activities. As a result, I developed high blood pressure and high blood sugar.

This moment led me to make significant changes. I began going to the gym, carving out more time for self-care, and working closely with both my medical doctors and functional medicine practitioners. I also continued my own healing work, and over time, my blood pressure and blood sugar levels improved. On top of that, I lost 40 pounds.

One powerful technique is to enter a meditative state, breathing in through your nose and out through your mouth. As you continue to breathe deeply, ask your blood pressure and blood sugar what they have to say to you. This practice helps you turn your attention inward instead of panicking about your diagnosis. Listen to what your body communicates and begin adjusting your life based on those insights. In my case, I clearly heard, "You make everyone else and everything else more important than me." This was my inner world speaking, acknowledging that I had been prioritizing everything and everyone above myself.

You can apply this same technique for any diagnosis. Simply go inward and listen, but one important point to remember is not to solidify the diagnosis. In my case, I say, "I was diagnosed as a diabetic," but I don't say, "I am a diabetic." By saying "I AM," you solidify the new program of diabetes in your body. Instead, by simply acknowledging the diagnosis as something that has occurred, you're not commanding it into existence. This distinction carries a different energy and emotion.

Was this process of changing my health immediate? Absolutely not. Depending on your own health situation, change can feel overwhelming. But you can begin by taking small steps. Much like any other challenge, health can seem like a mountain to climb, but you can only start where you are, taking it one step at a time. That's where the journey begins—with a single, intentional step forward.

The key is to honor your own path, trust the process of your healing, and recognize that each journey is unique.

The last thing I will say is that, since natural law governs the universe, it's crucial to understand that we cannot bypass it, especially because each of us has a different journey. This is what makes it so exciting—because as we live within the framework of natural law, it creates a unique experience for each of us based on the choices we make. I've found that when I embrace my sovereign mind, my life is filled with enrichment, happiness, fulfillment, joy, and peace. By aligning with these laws, we reconnect with our true nature and experience life in its fullest expression.

Honoring Yourself: The Foundation of Sovereignty

So far, I have shared many stories from my own life and the lessons I've learned. As I mentioned in the first part of this book, I learn from all aspects of my life, and my hope is that these lessons resonate with those who read them. However, my primary mission in this book is to fully express how I began to take my enslaved and codependent mind into a free and sovereign mindset. It's about transmuting oneself from an inner world of lead (heavy thoughts and energy) into gold (light thoughts and energy).

Through my own inner work, I've come to realize that the divine is not separate from me. I've experienced profound moments of connection with the source of life—whether you call it God, the Universe, or Spirit. As Hermetic philosophy suggests, "As above, so below; as within, so without." This teaches us that God is within us and all around us. We are the microcosm, and all that exists is the macrocosm. In truth, we are an aspect of all that is, and because we are an aspect, we are not separate from it. In a spiritual sense, we are also all that is because we are all one. When we align with the flow of all that is, we operate from a place of our highest and best good.

In previous chapters, I've shared with you the story of the apartment that manifested in my life in 2021, and how, after 26 months, I moved out right after returning from my trip to Scotland. I also talked about how busy and chaotic things were leading up to that trip and how hectic it was moving out of the apartment. What I haven't fully expressed is how I came to the decision to leave the apartment and what happened afterward.

Of course, my ego didn't want to move out. But as I sat and meditated on whether to stay or leave, I kept feeling an overwhelming force pushing me to move out. I tried focusing on different ways I could stay, but each time, it felt heavier inside. In truth, I probably could have stayed in the apartment, and based on my past, I would have found a way to make it work. But here's what pushed me over the edge—for the entire time I had been in this apartment, I had been processing a lot of emotional baggage. Leading up to the end of my consulting contract in August that year, I felt lighter than I had in a long time. But when I thought about staying in the apartment, a heavy feeling would wash over me. It felt almost like a current, pulling me away from it, a force that became almost unbearable.

I realized this was my soul pushing me in a direction. Yes, I had free will to stay, and yes, I probably could have made it work. But I had learned that if I didn't honor my inner world, I wasn't honoring the fullness of my life. The obvious truth is that the level of stress it would have taken to stay and make it work would have been too much. That kind of stress wasn't honoring myself.

The next step in this story takes us back to over a year before I moved out of the apartment. It was July 2022, and I was sitting on my couch with a friend who was visiting. We had been talking about a variety of topics and doing some deep spiritual work together, when suddenly, I felt a deep-rooted fear. The best way I can describe it is as a fear so profound, it felt as though it had built up over eons of time.

It was so powerful that it almost felt like it was shaking me apart from the inside.

If you remember, we've discussed conscious and subconscious feelings before. This fear was so deeply embedded within me that I wasn't consciously aware of it, other than the overwhelming sensation of shaking fear that coursed through me. I remember this feeling would resurface often over a four-month period in 2022, and I would simply sit and breathe through it. At one point, I walked around the apartment and said, speaking to the apartment itself, the furniture, and even down to the pots and pans, saying, "If you are not part of my divine plan, then I release you."

When I moved out and purged almost everything—fitting a 1,500 square foot apartment into a 10x10 storage locker—I also began to reflect on the people in my life. With love in my heart and soul, I said, "If you are no longer meant to be in my life, I lovingly release you." Sure enough, in September of that year, several people left my life. It was time for them to follow their own paths, and I needed to step into the life I was meant to live.

This kind of release allows you to move into a new stage of your life without being weighed down by things, people, or energies that are no longer part of your divine plan. It liberates and frees you—and it also liberates and frees them.

Fast forward to 2023, when I moved out of the apartment and with a friend to rent a room. My plan had been to travel, teach, and document my journey. I also intended to build a production company that created online webinars, alongside the Spirit Heart Cruise that we had started in 2018. However, this didn't happen as planned. Almost immediately after moving out, the momentum from my friend's podcast appearance faded, leaving just enough for me to cover my car payment, buy gas, and give me time to process everything that had happened.

I spent the next nine months continuing the work I had been doing for the past few years. But this time, whenever my mind or heart began to drift, I would pause and assess where I was. If my thoughts turned to worries about not having enough food or anything else, I knew I was projecting into the future, not living in the present moment. When we are not living in the present, our energy is out of balance, and we are not fully honoring ourselves at our highest and best good. If I became upset about past trauma, I recognized that I was stuck in the past, not in the present. In those moments, I would do the release work necessary to let go.

One tool I used was the Ho'oponopono prayer, a Hawaiian prayer that means, "I'm sorry, please forgive me, thank you, I love you." This prayer helps shift the focus of your thoughts from the past or future and releases them, allowing you to return to the present. When you are fully in the present moment, this is when you can truly manifest at a divine level.

There are several different techniques to help bring yourself back into the present moment, and over time, you will develop your own. But here are a few to get you started. Remember, for these techniques, you simply take a deep breath in through your nose and out through your mouth. Deep breathing helps change your brain frequency and allows effective change to occur within your energy.

When you start to stress about money or the lack of anything, try saying the following:

"Divine timing, divine plan, divine order, make it easy."

This phrase helps calm the mind as you breathe deeply. It's a reminder to God that you trust the process and that everything will unfold as it should and in the right order.

Spend time in nature and take in the calming breeze, the trees, the beautiful smells—just breathe and allow your mind to relax.

Prayer is powerful, but we don't need to beg. We need to be direct and precise about what we're praying for and remain open to receiving what serves our highest and best good.

Lastly, take time for yourself to simply be quiet. Let your mind rest and reconnect with your inner world.

I've shared this story because honoring myself meant following what I knew my soul was guiding me toward: a place where I could focus solely on working on myself, free from distractions and outside influence. Yes, I was still working on my coaching and speaking business, and yes, I was still doing the inner work, but what I truly discovered in 2024 was a deeper sense of myself than I had ever known before. From 2021 to the present moment, I've made several powerful commitments to myself and my soul.

Perhaps these statements will resonate with you.

- I will never let another person make me feel like I am a second option because I will never be a second option for myself again.
- I will never allow a job or any business situation to disrespect me because I know my own value and respect myself.
- I love everyone, and because I truly love myself, I understand that this means I will no longer accept situations that no longer serve my highest and best good.

Take some time to read these statements to yourself but really *feel* them as you take deep breaths in and exhale out. The idea is to ignite these commitments within your energy.

By making these statements, you are committing to serve your soul and God (which is not separate from you) to your highest and best good. When you commit to following the spirit within, you commit to your sovereignty. This spirit will guide you through life, and you will begin to feel a sense of peace within even when the world around you is full of chaos.

Take this path. It is the one that will be your savior because, in truth, *you are your own savior.* Nothing outside of you will save you, and nothing outside of you will bring you complete happiness or love.

When you honor yourself and live in alignment with your sovereign mind, the world around you will change. It will begin to manifest based on what is going on within you.

This journey can be difficult, but it is well worth the effort. The little over a year I spent after moving out of my apartment was, at times, incredibly stressful. I had moments of weakness and fear, but something deeper within assured me that I would be okay—and I was okay. I had a place to live, people who loved and supported me, and opportunities that just kept appearing. I ended up going on seven trips that year, which was part of my intention to travel.

This is where faith comes in. I was stressed about how things would work out, but every time an opportunity arose, I would say to God, "I know you've got my back." If I was meant to act on that opportunity, the universe would open itself to me. I remember my trip to California—at first, I wondered how I would afford the plane ticket, but then the money came in, and the ticket price dropped to something affordable.

The theme here is this: when you are direct with your request, and it is within your divine plan, nothing is too big for you. We have made our problems, our dreams, and life in general seem much bigger than ourselves. What we didn't understand is that it's the other way around: we are bigger than our problems, bigger than our dreams, and bigger than life itself. We operate within this three-dimensional framework, but we are the directors of our own movie.

Here's an even bigger lesson I learned in 2024, and it was not an easy one for me. I had always tried to bring my friends along with me, and if they couldn't afford to pay for what I wanted to do, I would do my best to cover the cost for them. In my mind, it didn't seem like a big deal. But in August of 2024, I lost another significant portion of my income as a learning and development consultant. Exactly one year after my last contract prematurely ended, a new one ended prematurely as well—and it happened just before I was set to finish paying off my cruise fare for the upcoming Spirit Heart Cruise.

I was also planning to pay for my friend to join us as our photographer. I realized I could still make it work, but it also felt like if I did, I would be creating more problems for myself. I had to make a difficult call and tell my friend that I couldn't afford to pay for them to come. It wasn't easy because I had built these cruises with the intention of sharing my love of travel with my friends.

Here's what I learned … we can still be generous at times, but if it doesn't work, it doesn't work. Trying to force something that's clearly going against the current flow is not honoring ourselves, and it may not be honoring our loved ones either.

We truly have no idea what not paying for someone might do for them, and here's how I came to this conclusion. I once had a boyfriend and a few friends who would make comments about me covering for them. I always thought I was being loving. In the end, that boyfriend ended up resenting me for being that person, and I was hurt because my intention was simply to make his life easier.

What I've learned, though, is that by covering for someone, we might be robbing them of the opportunity to gain the pride and strength it takes to pull themselves out of a difficult situation. This realization was further reinforced by the countless people I've coached who were navigating significant life changes—such as the loss of a partner or the beginning of a new journey after a divorce or separation. They were adjusting to doing things they'd never had to do before because their partner had always taken care of everything. I would help them through these times and then realized I had been doing the same thing.

It may have been a different circumstance, but when something is out of flow and making a partner uncomfortable, it's worth starting a conversation about it. Honoring ourselves means allowing ourselves to express our feelings—on both sides—in a healthy and open way, creating space for each person to grow in alignment with their soul. This is the essence of honoring yourself and others.

This is where clear boundaries come into play. Boundaries aren't just for other people—they are for us—to guide ourselves and help us navigate our interactions with the people we love. We've been misguided into thinking that self-care is simply about getting our nails done, hair styled, or taking a much-needed vacation. While these things certainly contribute to self-care, true self-care is about listening to that deeper voice within us and honoring what we feel on a profound level.

When we do this, we develop a healthy relationship with ourselves. We allow ourselves to express who we truly are, so we can share those deeper parts of ourselves authentically with those we interact with.

I want to end this chapter by inviting you to reflect on your own personal journey. Take a moment to think about and answer these questions:

- Do you feel empowered and inspired by the relationships you currently have in your life?
- Are any of these relationships causing you more stress than they bring you joy and empowerment?
- Do these relationships uplift you and challenge you to look within and become a better person?
- In your life right now, do you feel fulfilled and accomplished each night when you go to bed?
- Do you feel that you accomplished something toward your soul's growth each day?
- Do you feel stuck or hopeless in your current life?

If you answered yes to feeling stuck or hopeless, ask yourself why you feel this way. Where and when in your life did this feeling start? Let's break down these questions even further so we can learn how to process them.

Do you feel empowered and inspired by the relationships you currently have in your life?

This question invites you to reflect on the dynamics of all your relationships, not just romantic ones, but every relationship in your life. This includes your family, friends, romantic partners, work relationships, and anyone you interact with regularly. Some relationships challenge us to think and grow as individuals while others provide a sense of safety and welcome. Each relationship can bring a range of emotions.

One thing I know for sure is that all relationships should be built on mutual respect, allowing us to express our authentic selves. And when we can be our authentic selves, we are empowered and inspired.

Are these relationships causing you more stress than they bring you joy and/or empowerment?

I've shared how I've allowed certain behaviors in my life—watching people I cared about speak to me in hurtful ways, ignore me, or lie to me, while passing it off as my fault. What I've come to understand over the past 20 years is that when you express how you feel in a non-threatening way, most of the time, people genuinely want to change because they're unaware of how their actions affect you. When someone loves you, they typically don't want to continue hurting you.

I know this isn't always easy. We don't want to deal with the potential fallout when someone reacts negatively to us expressing how we feel. However, here's a question I'll leave with you. If someone reacts negatively to you by simply stating that their behavior or actions are hurting you, do you really want them to remain in your life? Honoring yourself isn't just about expressing your feelings when needed, it's also about walking away when someone repeatedly disrespects you and your boundaries.

Do these relationships uplift you or challenge you to look within and become a better person?

One of my closest friends has always challenged me, especially in the early stages of our friendship when I didn't fully understand myself. As we interacted, I would often get my feelings hurt due to the expectations I placed on them. When I started working on myself and setting boundaries, I noticed they began doing the same. We later apologized to each other for the things we said and did earlier in our friendship. As a result of both of us doing our individual work, we now share a healthy relationship. This dynamic allows us to express ourselves when we need to talk about something, listen without interrupting, joke and laugh together, and most importantly, feel a natural flow in our friendship.

I've seen similar transformations in my clients and other relationships in my life. But then, there are relationships that don't mutually grow. A friend of mine taught me this lesson over 20 years ago. She told me that if a relationship isn't growing mutually—where both parties are doing their inner work—then eventually, one will outgrow the other. At that point, you're left with a choice: walk away or stay.

When faced with this question, ask yourself: Does this friendship/relationship uplift me and/or make me a better person, or does it drag me down? If it drags you down with no hope of change in the future, it may be time to walk away. If the relationship is meant to stay in your life, it will return. But if it's not meant to be, why would you want it there?

Do you feel fulfilled and accomplished each night when you go to bed?

This was a hard lesson for me, and it wasn't until I became okay with being by myself and had truly built my relationship with the divine within me that I stopped feeling lonely. Once that shifted, I began feeling fulfillment every day because I felt inspired to do things that made my soul happy. This is why the inner journey is so crucial—it guides you toward a successful and fulfilled life.

Far too often, we look for things that don't fulfill us, such as the job that pays the most money but leaves us feeling miserable. I've seen this reflected in the many nurses and doctors I've worked with. They worked tirelessly on their education only to find themselves miserable in their fields. They initially chose their careers because they were stable and allowed them to help people but over time, they realized it wasn't the job that truly fulfilled them—and more importantly, it didn't make their soul sing.

Is there anything wrong with the pursuit of material objects? No, of course not but that's a conversation for another time. But the pursuit of material things solely for happiness is not the path we want to take. True fulfillment comes from exploring our inner world, and through that exploration, we find everything—including material things—aligned with our higher purpose.

Do you feel that you've accomplished something toward your soul's growth each day?

You will feel a sense of accomplishment each day when you are aligned with your soul, and it is in this alignment that your soul's purpose will begin to become clear. Many times, I have clients sitting in front of me that are feeling lost and trying to figure out their soul's purpose. The truth is, they won't fully discover their purpose until they establish a strong relationship with their soul. Once that connection is made, not only will their soul's purpose start to reveal itself but they will also experience the unification of their body, mind, and soul. This unification leads them to a profound understanding of their sovereignty.

So, begin working on your inner journey if you haven't already—or continue deepening the work you've begun. As you do, you'll not only uncover your true purpose, but you'll also begin to experience peace and fulfillment each day. This happens because, through self-awareness, you learn to accept and understand every aspect of your life. And it's in that acceptance that true peace is born.

Do you feel stuck or hopeless in your current life?

This question is a follow-up to the previous ones, and it's an area I find many people get stuck in when I work with them. This is where

I was at one point in my life, and it's where many of us end up. We feel frustrated, hopeless, and stuck, lost to the point where we have no idea where to begin.

So, let's start here. I want you to close your eyes for a moment and take a deep breath. Now, say to your whole being (your soul, your physical body, and everything that is you) the following statement: *"I want an open, honest, and healthy relationship with you. Through this relationship, I want to be motivated and inspired every day, allowing me to live in flow with you."*

How did that make you feel? Did you feel at peace as you said these words? Or did you feel stress in your body as you said? If you feel peace, that is a good sign, and it means you've already been directing your energy inward. If you felt stressed, it might indicate that you have trouble receiving this kind of honesty, especially from the most important person in your life: you.

This marks the beginning of honoring yourself. As we've already discussed, it all starts within, even when it comes to your physical health. A personal trainer once told me that fitness and health start in the kitchen—meaning that what you put into your body is a big part of your physical health.

Think about that for a moment: Do you eat what's convenient and cheap because it's the easiest? Or do you try to maintain healthy eating because you know it's better for you and your overall health? Everything starts within, and a lot of how we address our physical health reflects the energy within us.

Who is your priority? You or all the distractions around you? How we eat can affect our mood, energy, and health. While this book isn't about healthy eating, remember that your body is your temple, so be real—how do you want to honor it?

In reality, the fear I mentioned at the beginning of this chapter was the culmination of years of self-neglect. My subconscious knew I was about to face a huge blind spot in my life, and I was truly on the verge of transmuting my life into a higher state of being. For the physical body, that can be terrifying but it turned out to be the best thing I've ever done for myself.

Lastly, give yourself grace. You won't master this overnight. This book reflects over 25 years of work and self-discovery, and, in truth, it has been a lifetime of learning that led me to the point where I began writing. I made many mistakes along the way, and through those mistakes, I grew. So, instead of beating yourself up, give yourself grace. Flip the script and see it as an opportunity for growth—a chance to understand yourself on a deeper level so you can come home to yourself.

CHAPTER

7

Inspired Action: The Bridge to Manifestation

Like many of us, I once had a limited view of what success looked like. On a subconscious level, I believed asking for things wasn't spiritual or might even be selfish. As a result, I took a passive role in my prayers and intentions. Despite this perspective, amazing things still happened to me. For example, a friend and I once expressed how much we would love to go to concerts. Over the next six months, people kept handing us free concert tickets or inviting us to events where we could meet the bands and hang out.

While miraculous things can still happen when you're in a passive and receiving role, it's important to recognize that action is also required. You must be willing to act on the opportunities that come your way.

You can ask for what you desire, and this is clearly spelled out in this Bible verse:

> *"Ask, and it shall be given you; seek, and ye shall find; knock, and it shall be opened unto you: for everyone that asketh, receiveth; and he that seeketh, findeth; and to him that knocketh, it shall be opened."—Matthew 7:7-8*

I knew this passage well, but part of me also believed in the idea that "things will just be taken care of, and I don't need to worry about anything." This is a "love and light" mentality that suggests we don't need to set intentions or act toward those intentions. There's a common sentiment I hear among people—that we don't need to set intentions, we just need to find inner peace. While I agree with some of this sentiment, we must also remember that we are in these bodies to experience life as humans: the good, the bad, and the ugly. All of it.

Part of our healing journey is to examine all our limitations and ask for the highest and best good in our thoughts, intentions, and actions. When we begin to look at even the smallest, most subtle things, we can start to truly heal our inner world.

A recent experience highlighted this for me. Someone I love very much gave me a beautiful gift for my 51st birthday: a pair of black Christian Louis Vuitton boots with red rubber soles at the bottom. Now, I had no idea what "red bottoms" meant until I received these boots. Immediately, I was moved by the thoughtfulness of the gift. But then, I thought, "Wow, they spent so much on these," and I found myself spiraling into a fear-based story. I started to worry that people might judge me for being "too bougie" to be a spiritual teacher simply because I was wearing these boots.

The reality, however, was that I absolutely loved the boots. But I was starting to build a story of limitation in my mind until another friend shared her own experience with me. She told me how she used to hold herself back, thinking similar thoughts, and reminded me that we are here to enjoy life. The love and thoughtfulness that went into buying those boots for my birthday meant far more than the label on them.

What's more, I also feel good when I wear these boots. They make me feel classy, suave, and give me a more confident step in my walk. There are so many uplifting thoughts that run through my mind when I wear them, and most of those thoughts are rooted in the love and care of the person who gave them to me as a gift.

Here's the hard truth that some may not want to admit or hear: everything in life is spiritual. Everything. Yes, some of the decisions we make have consequences, and this is due to the law of cause and effect. It's not a punishment; it's simply a fact. When you hurt someone, something will eventually come around to show you that hurt. When you try to manipulate others into doing what you think is right, even with the best intentions, you are still manipulating another person. Eventually, the universe will show you that you are not working with the highest and best intentions.

This means we must be clear, honest, and direct about our intentions, something we've discussed throughout this book. So, how do you learn about cause and effect so you can truly understand it? You learn through your experiences. Honestly, you do it by making mistakes and realizing the impact of your decisions. The hope is that you will learn and grow from those mistakes. So, in truth, are they mistakes or opportunities?

No matter what we call them, you will never escape adversity in your life. It's impossible. I have clients tell me all the time that they can't wait to escape this planet because they can hardly take the world anymore. What they fail to see is that we will continue to cycle through our lessons until we finally understand them. And you want it to be this way because once you get the lesson, then you finally get it—and only then are you free from the bondage of the limiting programs you've been operating from.

What does this mean?

It means going out there and living. Ask for help—not only from the physical world, but from the spiritual world as well. When you ask in alignment with the highest and best good intention and allow your sovereign mind to guide you, you are standing in your full empowerment.

Reflection:

Let's take a few minutes to reflect on these questions:

- Do you cringe at receiving gifts from loved ones or anyone, even when it comes from an honest and loving place?

- If I were to ask you what you did today toward your dreams and goals, what would your response be? Would you share what you've accomplished, or would you list reasons why you did nothing?

- If I were to ask you to stand in front of the mirror and tell yourself how much you love yourself, how would that make you feel?

- If I were to ask you if you have any clarity about your dreams, or if you even know what they are, what would your response be?

- If I were to ask you if you clearly know who you are, what would the answer be?

- If I were to ask you if you were fully satisfied with your life and if you wake up each morning excited about the day and go to bed each night feeling accomplished and fulfilled— what would your answer be?

These are the questions I've asked myself since my first book, *Peace Be Still*, which was published 13 years ago. Yes, I had achieved a level of peace in my life, and I saw amazing things happening around me all the time. But I was still plagued by frustration about lacking, having to go back to work, and dealing with a whole lot of other things I was questioning in my life. It took me 13 years to truly understand this on a deeper level.

Before I dive into those realizations, there's another manifestation I want to share with you, one of many I want to tell you about. This happened this year, in the first two months of 2025.

I've been telling you about moving out of my dream apartment and into a friend's house for nine months. At the end of August 2024, I moved out of her house and began my couch surfing journey, planning to move up to Ocala to live with my cousin until I got back on my feet. I remember arriving at her house while she was in Pennsylvania, and I had a few days alone to really get quiet. During that time, I spent those days asking what I needed to do next.

I had just returned from the Abundant Soul event in Colorado Springs and was on an energetic high, but still not 100% clear on what I should be doing next. That's when I heard the message: Sit down to apply for jobs. I complied with the guidance and did just that—I applied for jobs.

A few days later, Hurricane Helene hit, and I felt strongly that I needed to head back down to the Tampa area to stay with my friends. This is where everything shifted. I ended up staying in Tampa to help my friends after the hurricane, and then I got a call from one of the jobs I had applied for. I had an interview with them, and after just one interview, I got the job.

Now, let me tell you—my career has never involved just one interview. It's usually stretched out over a minimum of three interviews, sometimes four, five, or even a total of eight before I receive an offer. So, when I got the call that I had the job, only three days after the first interview, I was both surprised and happy.

This is a crucial part of the journey: aligning with your higher purpose, taking inspired action, and watching how the universe supports you in return. The flow of your dreams depends on your willingness to act in faith and clarity.

It took me a few weeks to get started because Hurricane Milton delayed my plans. During this time, I was invited by friends to stay with them, including one who owned several Airbnbs. For a few months, I stayed in properties of hers that had vacancies.

All the while, I kept feeling compelled to apply for a specific apartment complex. I hesitated, unsure if it was the right time, especially when I was repeatedly told there was a year-long wait list. I let this hesitation linger until early February. Finally, I submitted the application, visited a model unit, and was told the same thing— that it would take up to a year for a unit to become available.

I specifically asked for a two-bedroom apartment with a washer and dryer, and a lake view. Just one week later, I received a call saying they had an available apartment—but I had to move in within a week.

The stress was overwhelming—preparing for the next Spirit Heart Cruise, organizing the upcoming Inner Temple Symposium, and managing about 20 speaking engagements. On top of that, I was teaching a class online for four different countries in my day job. I wasn't even sure who would help me move.

But I paused, took a breath, and said: Divine timing, divine order, divine plan—make it easy—while visualizing, and most importantly, feeling how smoothly everything would unfold. Sure enough, I had the help I needed to move, and by mid-February, I was settled into my new apartment.

I share this story because it highlights a few important principles.

First, I followed my inner voice and waited for the right moment to apply. I didn't force it. I allowed the timing to unfold naturally. When the moment came, I acted without hesitation—even though it felt stressful and nearly impossible. And because of that, I asked for help and received it exactly when it was needed.

This is why the questions I raised earlier are so vital. When you can get clear with these questions and eliminate any limitations, you align with your sovereign mind. That's when things begin to manifest on a higher, faster level.

Let's explore these questions more deeply.

Do you cringe at receiving gifts from loved ones even when they come from an honest and loving place?

We touched on this in a previous chapter, but I feel it's worth revisiting. If you cannot freely receive, you may be blocking blessings from God. This isn't just about gifts—it extends to compliments, acts of kindness, and more.

Think about someone telling you that you are beautiful or handsome. Do you accept the compliment graciously, or do you get embarrassed and wonder why they would say that, not seeing what they see in you?

It's time to change that inner dialogue. Say to yourself, while taking deep breaths in and exhaling out, and telling yourself, *"I graciously accept all the blessings that are given to me. Just as I give freely from the heart, I also receive just as freely. By doing so, I create a flow of blessings and abundance for myself and all those I come into contact with. It is time."*

If I were to ask you what you did today toward your dreams and goals, how would you respond?

Would you share your accomplishments or would you list reasons why you did nothing? I understand. We work, raise kids, manage relationships, and juggle countless responsibilities. There's so much to do and so little time. And when we do have time, we're often exhausted. I get it.

But let me offer a different perspective. At the end of your life, what do you want your legacy to be? What do you want your loved ones or children to remember about you? Do you want them to see someone they love dearly—someone who gave them an example of life's possibilities? Do you want them to dream big and act on those dreams, or simply wish and never achieve?

I've asked myself these same questions. I spent years doing things for others, committing to them, but never working on myself or my dreams. One day, I made a commitment to take at least one step each day toward my goals—no matter how small.

I also learned the importance of grace, understanding that I couldn't do everything at once. Much like the Law of Gestation, I knew it would take time to give birth to the new version of myself that I envisioned.

This journey requires sacrifice. So, what are you willing to sacrifice today to achieve your goals? And when will you start?

Remember, nothing happens if you do nothing. But even small actions create momentum in the universe. They send a message to God, saying, "I'm working on myself." Over time, as you take action, you'll peel back layers and discover more about who you truly are. Action, combined with intention, creates transformation. So, take some action, no matter how small, every day.

If I were to ask you to stand in front of the mirror and tell yourself how much you love yourself, how would that make you feel?

As we discussed in a previous chapter, this exercise makes many people uncomfortable. But at its core, it's about receiving. If you can't receive love from yourself, how can you receive love from others?

By practicing this simple exercise, you'll begin a journey of self-discovery. As you look into your own eyes and express love, things will begin to surface—things you thought you had forgotten, or things you had no idea still bothered you. This is the beginning of your journey toward self-acceptance, which marks the start of a new era for you.

The best part is it takes little physical effort—other than the discomfort you may feel. And that discomfort is a good thing. Getting out of your comfort zone is exactly how you will change your life.

Are you ready?

If I were to ask you if you have clarity on your dreams or even know what they are, what would your response be?

I receive a variety of answers when I ask this question to my clients or anyone seeking guidance. Many say they have a dream but no plan of action. Others know they want change but are unsure how to make it happen. A common response is the desire for more money and security, thinking this will lead to freedom. This is one of the most frequent answers I hear. Many people also mention wanting freedom and fulfillment.

Here's the truth: freedom starts with freeing yourself from the limiting thoughts you create every day. It's about breaking free from the programing you've been given and the voices in your mind telling you what success should look like.

Success is defined by you, but I can almost certainly tell you that it's not defined by money. Yes, money helps us pay for things and helps achieve dreams, but as you free yourself from limiting thoughts and pursue a dream that truly makes you happy, abundance will flow in. When you choose yourself and commit to your happiness, things will begin to fall into place. But this requires daily action on your part.

If I were to ask you if you clearly know who you are, what would your answer be?

We are much deeper beings than we often acknowledge. Too often, we get caught up in the world around us and lose sight of who we truly are—that we are spiritual beings having a human experience. So, who are you? Do you know?

While many of you may identify as parents, friends, healthcare workers, healers, or other labels, *who are you really?* The answers to these questions can only be found by journeying inward.

In 2010, I met a group of friends who made me feel like a teenager again. We laughed, were silly, and played games together. It was with them that I finally began to practice how I wanted to be. I started to express my authentic self, and as I peeled back the layers, I began to understand who I truly was—on a deeper, more soulful level. It begins by asking yourself the hard questions and facing who you are—and who you are not.

Are you fully satisfied with your life? Do you wake up excited about the day and go to bed feeling accomplished and fulfilled?

If not, what would it take to reach that level of satisfaction?

As much as some of you may not want to hear this, it begins with going within to face yourself and all the programing and messages you've internalized. It starts with creating a connection with your soul and embracing your sovereign mind.

This is not an overnight process. It took you years to become who you are right now, and it will take time to unravel the life you've lived to transform into the freedom you seek. This is because we must first unravel the "slave mindset" we've unconsciously created.

This chapter is about action and how it bridges the gap to manifestation. It's easy to share stories of people who took action and manifested a beautiful life, but I believe that if you don't embrace the spiritual principles of inner discovery, any manifestation will feel temporary. Why? Because your manifestations may become distractions from the real part of yourself.

Take my experience manifesting the vice president position, for example. I took action. I had intention. But when I reached that position, I didn't like it. This is where asking for the highest and best good becomes crucial.

The real action you need to take is to discover why you are not fully connected to your soul. Once you uncover that, you can set clear intentions, take purposeful action, and feel the effects—not just on your physical self, but on your soul. This is when things will truly start to manifest because when you are in full alignment with your body, mind, and soul, everything begins to flow.

Turning Faith into Knowing

8

Typically, when I thought of faith, I associated it with religion. However, I've come to understand that faith is much more than just a religious concept. It is, in fact, a deeply spiritual idea. Spirituality, in my view, is a personal journey that each of us takes throughout our lives. Along this journey, we discover what resonates with us— not only on a physical level but also on a spiritual one. When these two aspects of our being work together in unison, we begin to experience peace in our lives. This journey requires faith—the faith to step into the unknown in search of that peace.

A perfect example of this is the bond between a child and its parents. A newborn has inherent faith and trust that its needs will be met and that it will be kept safe. This trust forms the foundation of the child's relationship with the world, allowing it to experience life fully, knowing it is supported. The relationship between the child and its caregivers is built through the parent's actions and the environment surrounding the child from an early age.

In many ways, our journey through life mirrors this process. We take steps forward without always knowing how things will unfold, but to grow, we must take leaps of faith. It's through these leaps that we evolve into better versions of ourselves.

A big lesson many of us learn is that sometimes, we must take that leap to free ourselves—so we can eventually soar—like the mother bird pushing her chick from the nest. For the offspring to spread its wings, it must first be pushed out of its comfort zone. Similarly, we need to be pushed out of our own comfort zones at times to move past complacency. While complacency may feel comfortable, we must be honest with ourselves: it does not usually breed fulfillment. Only when we take risks, face discomfort, and push forward do we truly experience growth and fulfillment in our lives, and this will eventually lead us to a life full of peace and happiness. And of course, until that happens, we will seek happiness and enjoy the moments we have right now.

An interesting thing happened as I started to write this chapter on faith. It was a strange experience, yet very realistic to life because it's my life and my journey as I write these pages. I want to share this with you in the hope that it will inspire you to reflect on your own life and ask yourself: How are you blocking the joy that could come into your life by following your inner guidance?

As I began writing about faith, my mind became blocked, much like it had been for the past 13 years as I waited to write this book. Thoughts of not being good enough resurfaced. I feared how I would get this book into people's hands so it could touch their lives. Imposter syndrome kicked in hard, and for over a week, I couldn't write anything. Then, I felt my inner voice saying exactly what I would say to someone else: "Get quiet, get still, and listen."

As I attempted to do just that—spend time getting quiet—I found myself procrastinating, even on the smallest tasks like washing the dishes or going to the gym. All I wanted to do other than work was lay around and watch television. I'd force myself to turn off the TV to get quiet, but then I'd catch myself picking up my phone and diving down a rabbit hole of useless internet searches that had nothing to do with writing this chapter on faith.

I've been through countless situations where my faith proved to be exactly the route I needed because everything worked out in its own time. But this year, 2025, has been an interesting, wonderful, and heavy one—full of emotions, discoveries about myself, and processing thoughts, feelings, and ideas I hadn't even considered in a long time. I've discovered new things about my mother, mourned the passing of my cousin from cancer, and experienced a lot in a short amount of time. Faith was on my mind and heart, as I turned inward to pray for guidance, knowing everything would work out in the end.

So, why did I feel this heaviness inside? The same type of heaviness I felt as a teenager or young adult, thinking I was a disappointment to others. This realization hit me hard in the last week of processing this chapter. Imposter syndrome was still present—not a lack of faith in God, spirit, the universe, or whatever you want to call the higher power—but a lack of faith in myself. I doubted my ability to convey the message I had wanted to express for so long in a book. The range of emotions, doubts, and energy swirling in my mind became overwhelming, and I started slipping into old familiar habits.

Then one night, during meditation and prayer, I heard the message: "Be honest in this chapter about how you're feeling and the imposter syndrome you're experiencing."

At first, I didn't fully understand why I needed to express and be vulnerable about what has been going through my mind and heart while writing this chapter. However, as I sat down and the words began to flow across the page, I realized that vulnerability is, in fact, an expression of faith. It's not only faith in myself but also faith in the divine, in the people who will read this book, and in the lives that will be touched.

If there's one thing I've learned in life, it's that people respect honesty. We all crave the reassurance that others are experiencing similar struggles—whether it's pain, anxiety, or self-doubt—and that we're not alone in those feelings. We all face moments of fear—fear of failure, fear of losing everything, and fear of the unknown. And in those moments, it's comforting to know that we share this human experience, and we are not isolated in our challenges.

As I've mentioned before, this book has been a journey of truly getting to know my inner world, so that both my inner and outer worlds can finally work in unison. This harmony is what forms the sovereign mindset we all have within us. And the only way to accomplish this is by having faith in the journey you are on—faith that it will lead you to discover, heal, and ultimately bring about that union.

I'm sure, like me, you have countless stories of times when you took a leap of faith and things worked out in the end. And there have likely been times when things didn't work out exactly the way you wanted—but at the end of the day, you were still here, still living, and able to try again.

Things working out aren't always about getting what we want—often, it's about receiving what we truly need. Faith shows up in those moments when everything feels like it's falling apart or not going the way we expected. It helps us exercise that inner muscle, encouraging us to take leaps even in uncertainty.

Faith builds a stronger foundation within us as we act on our intentions. And over time, those leaps of faith create a life we can look back on with pride.

I've coached many people who were unhappy in their lives and wanted to make a change within themselves. It takes tremendous courage to step away from the life you've always known to create a life more aligned with your purpose.

I remember in 2019, my business partner and I had our very first Spirit Heart Cruise, where 126 people joined us on an incredible seven-day journey. On that cruise, I formed lifelong friendships with several of the attendees. I recall feeling that it was going to change my life forever, and it did. It was during that event that I began to see my work as a business, not just a hobby.

That was the moment I began to shift the way I approached my spiritual work. I started to reassess how I was living my life, what I was prioritizing, and the relationships I was nurturing. From that point on, I began forming new friendships, letting go of relationships that no longer serve my highest good, and transforming how I viewed myself when I looked in the mirror.

As I made different choices, my self-esteem grew stronger, my passion for my work deepened, and I was on a journey of self-discovery I had never experienced before. I watched those around me go through similar transformations, letting go of people and situations that no longer served them, much like I was doing. This is the path to truly discovering who we are, and as we've clearly stated, it's the only path we can take to achieve full wholeness in our lives.

As we take action and make different choices, our lives evolve and so do the people around us. This process brings new opportunities, new choices, and new experiences. It all begins with learning how to prioritize yourself and develop that essential relationship with yourself. As you begin to grow, you will gain a solid understanding of yourself in various areas of your life, and eventually, there will no longer be "faith"—there will be knowing. When you approach new areas of life that are unfamiliar to you, that's when you'll rely on faith, just as you have in the past.

I recall a conversation with a friend in 2012. He was surprised at how quickly I managed to secure new jobs, while others struggled. I would often find a new position shortly after beginning my job search. There have been more than a few instances where I simply declared it was time for a change, or that I needed a new job and it would appear almost instantly.

One such instance was when I prayed, asking for a new opportunity. Within 24 hours, I received an email from a woman I had applied with seven years prior. She had a position open, offering $20,000 more per year than I had been making. I applied and was hired.

Another instance was when I went to work for an accounting firm. I had just lost a significant portion of my income, and I remember lying down, praying, and asking for clarity on my next opportunity— one that would come easily and be obvious. Less than 45 minutes later, I received a call from a recruiter who had seen an old resume of mine on Indeed. He had been trying to get in touch with me. I ended up working there for three years as the training manager.

So, my friend was right. I did not typically have trouble getting a job when I was clear on what I wanted and I was willing to receive my next opportunity and yes, these things came in literally that fast but when it's not something we are used to or it takes us out of our comfort zone, this is when faith becomes a key component to our next steps in a new journey. This is when you must remind yourself that you not only been taken care of each time you have gone out on a limb so to speak but you have also been successful as you have jumped into new paths in your life. The real truth is that not making changes in your life will not allow you to optimize who you are as a person and as a soul.

I had a friend tell me about the word God and she broke it down like this—that God is goodness over doubt and basically, it is the goodness in you that overcomes the doubt in you. This is powerful because our brains will go into doubt out of fear because we are going into areas that are unfamiliar to us, but we must allow that goodness in us to rule so that we can overcome that doubt when it happens. Doubt can only be washed away through action, and this requires us to have faith in our abilities to navigate new areas of our life.

The next step in faith is essential, and it's important because we've discussed a great deal about manifesting the world around us and how we need to change our inner world to truly manifest the external world we desire. Here's a major reason why.

I've studied many of the major religions of the world, as well as numerous books on manifestation. A common theme across all of them—from Christianity to New Thought, Wicca, and others—is that you pray, do a ritual, or set an intention (such as creating a vision board) using whatever medium resonates with you. However, there is one critical element that most of us struggle with: **letting go** once we've set the intention.

I remember once when I set an intention and was actively working toward it. I kept asking spirit if it was going to happen, and the response was, "*No, it's not going to happen because you don't really believe it will.*" I was taken aback by this answer because I had previously felt so confident that I was on the right path, certain that I was doing exactly what I was meant to do.

Then came the epiphany. Yes, you are on the right path, but by repeatedly asking whether it will happen, you are not truly having faith that things will work out in the highest and best way. By setting your intention, and then continuing to ask, your energy is feeding doubt, which sets you back in your ability to manifest what you desire. In essence, it's like pressing the brake while also pressing the gas pedal to the floor. Your energy is trying to move in two different directions, and nothing is really happening.

This is where faith comes into play. You set your intention with a clear vision, and then you let it go. From there, you act on the opportunities that present themselves, knowing that action creates movement.

The lesson here is simple yet profound: **Set your intention, then let it go.** Don't obsess over it. Instead, work toward it, live as if you've already achieved it, and act on opportunities that align with your vision when they resonate with you. Trust and listen to your inner guidance along the way.

Let's look at where we are in terms of our faith muscle by gaining self-awareness through these deeper questions:

- Do you trust the people closest to you, or are you always waiting for the other shoe to drop?
- Do you set out to accomplish something, only to worry or obsess about whether you're on the right path?
- Do you constantly see a person in the mirror that you're ashamed of or criticize? Or, when you see your reflection, are you proud of what you see?
- Who do you turn to when faced with a problem that can't be solved by physical means?
- Do you have a solid relationship with whoever you pray to?
- Are you satisfied with your life? If not, what do you do daily to change the circumstances of your life?

I truly believe that all of us have something to work on, and that we all carry some form of limitation within our thoughts. These limitations are often tied to something we're holding onto whether it be an idea that no longer serves us, a toxic relationship, or a past pain or hurt. As a result, these limitations sit within our energy, preventing us from moving forward in our lives. When we let go and take a step forward, we begin the journey of moving into the future and releasing the past.

Let's break these questions down.

Do you trust the people closest to you, or are you always waiting for the other shoe to drop?

I always considered myself a trusting person. Then, when I found myself in a new relationship, I noticed feelings of jealousy arose whenever I didn't hear from them right away. I'd also be watching television shows and when a certain situation reminded me of past hurts, I could feel that old pain resurface. As the circumstances would change, I realized I was overreacting to something fictional.

This made me realize a pattern in my own life. I was letting my past guide me instead of living fully in the present moment. In that moment of clarity, I knew it was time to begin transmuting the energy within me. Too often, I, like many others, made excuses, telling myself, "This is just who I am." But that's not true. Who we truly are is a pure, beautiful soul who deserves happiness and fulfillment. We can find that happiness by appreciating who we are and cherishing our interactions with the people we love.

True fulfillment comes from setting appropriate boundaries and expressing ourselves in ways that allow us to be vulnerable, open, and honest about who we are and what we're going through. This is where true emotional freedom begins and where we start healing toxic patterns. But this fulfilment process takes faith in ourselves (and others) to stay open and vulnerable in the process.

Do you set out to accomplish something only to worry or obsess about whether you're on the right path?

Some might argue that this happens because they care deeply about what they're trying to accomplish. I can understand that perspective, but I see it a little differently—especially when we consider how energy flows within the body. When you stress about whether something will work out, it's as if you're telling the universe that you want to act with intention, setting energy in motion toward your desire.

However, at the same time, you're also sending a mixed signal—communicating doubt and a lack of trust in the outcome. This energetic contradiction creates resistance, blocking the natural flow of energy and, in turn, hindering the manifestation process.

Do you constantly see a person in the mirror that you're ashamed of or criticize? Or, when you see your reflection, are you proud of what you see?

The question I eventually had to ask myself, and what I present to my clients, is this: Who gave you the perception you have about yourself? Who told you that you are not something to be proud of—physically, mentally, and spiritually? Where did that idea come from? Was it your own idea, or did it come from others telling you that you're not good enough? Did it come from kids at school, co-workers, employers, friends, family, or your church? Do you look in the mirror and think you're too fat? Too skinny? Who told you any of this? I can almost guarantee it didn't start with you.

Now, I'm not here to say that we shouldn't take steps to better ourselves because, like all of you, I've worked on myself, stopped working on myself, been successful at it, and at times not so successful. I've come to understand the deeper reasons why I now care for my health. I go to the gym, eat better, and focus on taking care of myself—not for the approval of others, but for me. And this is what you want to do—make these choices for you and your own health.

The truth is, when we do these things seeking approval or acceptance from others, we're setting ourselves up for major disappointment. Why? Because in those moments, we're doing it for someone else, not for ourselves. I've lost weight and gained weight throughout my adult life, and I've had people tell me they found me more attractive when I had more weight on me—and others who preferred me when I had less. Physical attraction is always based on the perceptions of others.

That's why it's so important to turn inward, build a solid relationship with ourselves, and make choices for us, not for anyone else.

Who do you turn to when faced with a problem that can't be solved by physical means?

This was a hard question for me because I was raised by a single mother, and due to attending over 30 different schools growing up, I didn't start forming real bonds with people my age until high school. I became accustomed to doing things on my own, and the only person I truly turned to was my mother. When she passed away in 2012, I would turn to her in the spiritual realm, but not surprisingly, it just wasn't the same.

As I reflected on all the experiences I've shared in this book, I began to realize that there was a force working in my favor. When I asked, I generally received—and often at a level much greater than I had ever planned or envisioned. That's when it truly occurred to me: this force, which some might call God or the Universe, is guiding us, helping us, and loving us at every level of our lives. I have experienced this truth over and over again.

When we turn to this force, we begin to see profound changes in our lives, changes that bring us situations far more fulfilling than we could have ever imagined. This is why it's so important to cultivate the daily practice of going within, connecting with this force deep inside us, and asking for help when we need it.

Do you have a solid relationship with whoever you pray to?

If you consider yourself spiritual in any way, you likely have some form of spiritual practice—whether it's meditation or prayer. To be honest, I believe both are essentially the same, as they involve quieting the mind and connecting with the force that is creating with you.

But here's the thing—you don't have to label yourself spiritual to benefit from quieting your mind. For years, I've encouraged my clients not to worry about whether they're doing meditation or doing prayer but instead to simply focus on being still with themselves.

Of course, some people resist this. They'll say they can't stand the silence because it drives them crazy or they don't want to face what comes up when they get quiet. And that's exactly why stillness is so important because it gives us the chance to face the inner thoughts we've been avoiding.

It's vital to cultivate a solid relationship with this part of ourselves. As we've discussed before, when we begin to work in unison with our soulful essence, we start living as sovereigns in our own lives. Self-doubt fades, clarity emerges, and we begin moving through life in flow, fully present in the now.

This process requires understanding, vulnerability, and the courage to heal the sources of pain and stagnation that keep us from living our fullest lives.

Are you satisfied with your life? If not, what are you doing daily to change the circumstances of your life?

I often receive a variety of long-winded answers to this question, but I challenge my clients to keep it simple. I ask them for a yes or no answer to this question "Are you happy with your life?"

I understand that this question can make us uncomfortable because it forces us to be honest with ourselves. It also compels us to examine why, if our answer is "no," we aren't happy. What are we holding onto that prevents us from experiencing happiness? What changes do we need to make in our lives to create happiness? Or what do we need to confront and release—whether it's old hurts, patterns, situations, or relationships—to find that happiness?

I encourage you to stand in front of a mirror and ask yourself, "Are you happy?" Be honest with yourself. This question is meant to open areas within you that may have been left unexamined for a long time.

Faith is like a muscle, it grows through the process of looking inward, taking leaps of faith, and practicing vulnerability and acceptance while staying true to yourself. It means showing up for yourself every day and committing to your personal growth and healing.

Just like working out your physical muscles, the more you use faith, the stronger it becomes. And if you neglect it, that muscle can weaken and eventually atrophy from lack of use.

Asking yourself these hard questions (and others you can devise for your situation) will help you dig deeper into the root of what's going on. Give yourself grace and understanding. We all have opportunities to grow and better understand ourselves.

Have faith in the process. As you continue to follow it, you'll eventually reach a place of deep knowing that everything is taken care of. Things may not unfold exactly the way you want them to, but you can trust that they will always happen for your highest and best good.

Clarity of Intention: The Key to Manifesting Desires

One thing I've noticed with many clients I work with is that their energy and thoughts are all over the place. They have a desire to set an intention and work toward something they want but then they become unsure if that's the right path. This is what I call "cross-purposing." Their desire is focused in one direction, but it gets pulled in another due to old habits and programs.

When I work with my clients, I ask them what they feel they should do, trying to gauge where their thoughts are. The answers I receive are varied but many express feelings of being torn, confused, unsure, and sometimes completely lost about what they should do next. They struggle to understand their purpose in life. Most are filled with ideas about how life should be but the truth is, many of these ideas aren't their own; they're based on what others have told them.

This is where the real work begins. We need to take time to get to the root of who we truly are so we can fully understand our own authentic thoughts. As we peel back the layers, we discover how disempowered they've been by others' ideas and experiences throughout their lives.

One of the most rewarding experiences is as when you peel back the layers you start to see where you have held yourself back because of your own limitations. You begin to see that life will unfold in a fashion that helps you awaken your true self and that's a union with all aspects of who we are. This brings us to a point where manifestation really can happen to be our highest and best self.

I've worked with countless people who are amazing souls yet they feel torn by the ideas and expectations placed upon them. When they begin to examine these ideas, they realize they were not their own. Instead, they were shaped by society, friends, and loved ones—ideas that weren't born from their own experiences.

One prevalent belief is that while we are children of God, we are also sinners, and that our flesh is flawed. Yes, the flesh is flawed, but we are not just flesh. We are so much more than the physical body we inhabit every day. This is the missing piece in that teaching. The real definition of sin is "missing the mark," and when you think about aligning with your soul, this makes perfect sense. It means we are missing the mark when we are not properly aligned with our soul.

As a physical body, we don't have the foresight that our souls possess. But when we unify these two energies—our physical and spiritual selves—this shifts. The result is that our cross-purposing and self-doubt begin to fade away.

The key to manifesting the life you desire is to declare your intention with absolute confidence, then let it go. Take action to create momentum around that intention. The stories I've shared throughout this book happened because in those moments, I clearly declared my intention with my whole mind, heart, and spirit—and then things unfolded. In other times, when I was uncertain or wishy-washy, things manifested, but not exactly as I had hoped, and often led me to challenges.

So, here are the steps to manifesting your desires:

1. **Get clear about what you want.** Be specific. Visualize what you want to manifest in your life and feel what it would be like to already be living that reality.

2. **Breathe deeply.** As you visualize, take deep breaths in through your nose and out through your mouth, allowing yourself to relax into the process.

3. **Pay attention to your thoughts and feelings.** Are they being triggered by limitations? Do you feel stress in your body as you work through this process? Those are your energy blocks. That's the fearful, limited mind coming up with programs that say, "This isn't possible" or "You're being foolish."

4. **Acknowledge and coach yourself.** Gently tell yourself, "If this is meant to be, then make it easy."

5. **Affirm divine timing and order.** Say in your mind and heart: "Divine timing, divine plan, divine order, make it easy." As you say this, continue to breathe deeply, allowing your mind and body to relax.

6. **Let it go.** Trust that the energy will do its work. Know that it will bring you exactly what is for your highest and best good, in divine timing and divine order.

I've provided these steps because the logical, left-brain side of us often wants structure. But I'm going to be completely honest—what I truly want you to do is feel this process and allow your inner world to guide you through it.

If you get too caught up in following the steps, you'll limit yourself. Why? Because steps and processes are inherently limiting, and they keep you energetically confined to a box. You are anything but limited.

Use these steps to get started but then let your inner world take the lead. Allow it to guide you as you peel back the layers and discover more about yourself.

What's important to understand is the need to really look at what's going on within you. Where is your energy? Where are your thoughts and emotions? Think of your body as a manifesting generator. Since it is the focal point for the manifestations in your world, it's essential to ensure that your body is in balance. If your energy is too fixated on one thing or scattered across too many things, it won't be operating at its optimal level.

Here are some things to consider:

- **Energy Focused on Negativity**

  If your energy is consumed by worrying about the state of the world or constantly focused on what's wrong, your energy becomes seeded with ideas of misery and fear. As a result, misery will manifest around you. This is when it's important to look at why you're in a negative state of mind. What can you do to shift it, both in the short term and long term?

- **Judgmental Energy**

  If your energy is constantly stressed about being judged by others or the world, you will create a reality where you feel perpetually judged. This is why inner work—learning to love and accept yourself authentically—is so essential. Remember, just be authentically you because at your core, there is only one you, and the world needs you to be exactly that.

- **Financial Stress**

  Are you constantly stressed about the future and how you'll make ends meet financially? Do you feel anxiety when bills arrive in the mail or are you afraid to check your bank account? It all starts by examining your relationship with money. I understand that you might be in a difficult financial situation, as I've been there myself. However, it begins by facing your current financial reality, showing gratitude for where you are right now, and then taking small, intentional steps toward changing your situation, one step at a time.

- **Tension During Intentions**

  When you set an intention or pray for something, do you feel tension in your energy, a heaviness or experience thoughts of doubt? These are energy blocks and programs within your body that signal a limited viewpoint about money. These feelings may stem from past experiences or deeply held beliefs. This is where the work begins—analyzing your relationship with money and your perception of it. Do you see money as the root of all evil? Do you have beliefs like "money doesn't grow on trees" or that a spiritually minded person shouldn't have money?

  Start by questioning these limiting beliefs. Do you really believe them? Who told you these beliefs? Did they come from within you, or were they handed down by someone else?

It's natural, due to our conditioning and internal programming, to worry about these things. However, I want to offer a perspective for you to consider. If you are worrying about things, you cannot control or things you're unwilling or unable to do anything about, why are you allowing such stress into your life?

I'm specifically referring to things we see in the news. Yes, I understand that we want to stay informed about what's happening in the world, but at the same time, we must be mindful of where our energy is being directed.

When you witness a tragedy, it's natural to feel compassion. But if you allow your energy to remain stuck in that tragedy, it lowers your vibration and causes you to stay immersed in that emotional state, and that's where you lose balance.

I have spent hundreds of hours studying how the brain works, how energy functions, and how we can create and manifest the world around us. But it wasn't until I started getting quiet and really paying attention to where my energy was focused throughout the day that things began to click.

For most of my life, there was always a part of me that felt suppressed with thoughts of not being good enough, believing everyone else had what I didn't—whether it was being smarter or further along in life. I was unknowingly creating a world around me that constantly reflected those beliefs.

However, when I started to get quiet and truly tune into where my energy was, I discovered a gentle voice—a subtle feeling guiding me along my journey. This voice and feeling would lead me to meet new people who would say something that clicked for me, serving as breadcrumbs along the path, continuously guiding me in the right direction.

I remember one specific conversation with a woman I met. She shared a message about a group of people I was involved with. She told me that this phase would soon end but that it would be a good thing even though it might hurt. She said this change would ultimately send me in the direction I needed to go.

Sure enough, six months later, I faced exactly what she had predicted. That moment was the catalyst for transforming my life into one that was more soul-fulfilling.

The lesson I got from this was that anything that belongs to your soul divinely can never be taken away from you. So, if it's meant to be in your life, then it will come back or will never leave. However, if it is not yours, then why would you want it in your life? It hit me one day speaking on a stage while I was talking about these lessons and I said, "This is what you will always want to remember, that when you are in alignment and you are operating in your sovereign mindset, then you will know what to do, when to do it, where to be and how to do it. You will know what to say and how to say it all at the right and perfect time."

After this presentation, I started saying these thoughts to myself every time I would worry about something, knowing that I was countering the worry with a new program of assurance in my mind and energy.

This is when a new version of my inner conversation made a significant shift. I began telling myself whenever certain thoughts would pop up and when I would stress about money, that it was important to breathe deeply and remind myself that I would have what I need at the time I needed it for the things I divinely need to pay in divine timing.

This affirmation was a reminder that if I was meant to pay something, it would be paid at exactly the right time. And this worked.

I did, however, go through a period of hardship, and during that time, I had to remind myself of those words. I would tell myself that I would pay what I needed to pay in divine timing, and it suddenly hit me—when I am able to pay something, I will—if I can, and if I could not, I would let it go and do my best.

Notice that this phrase isn't about neglecting your commitments, but rather about letting go and trusting that, at the highest level, you are taken care of. If you're going through significant loss, understand that it's guiding you toward the direction that's best for your soul. This process of letting go allows your energy to be fully present in the moment, enabling you to appreciate where you are right now. By doing so, you align with the knowing that everything will unfold and be taken care of in divine timing.

This shift helps change your energy from feeling heavy with worry to feeling grounded, knowing that you will do your best to take care of things in a timely manner while also surrendering the energy to let it unfold in divine timing. Recognizing that divine timing might come sooner—or even better than we expect—reminds us that when we release expectations, we free ourselves to embrace the flow of life.

This leads me to one of the final points of this chapter, which centers around the idea of divine timing and divine order. Let's begin with a quick exercise. Find a comfortable position and relax your body. Take a deep breath in through your nose and exhale slowly through your mouth. Do this a few times, making sure your breaths are gentle and slow, almost as if you are calming a scared child or puppy. This is you soothing your own mind with the same tenderness you would offer to someone else in need.

As you continue to breathe, begin to focus your attention on your dreams, desires, and goals. Visualize them in your mind and feel them in your heart. Do they bring you happiness, peace, and joy? Allow yourself to feel those emotions as if you are experiencing them right in this moment. With each breath, imagine gently spreading these positive feelings throughout your body—from the tips of your fingers and toes, all the way up to your head. As you continue, feel your energy expanding, filling the space around you with those good, positive emotions.

Take your time with this exercise. As you continue to hold this space of good feelings in your body and the energy field around you, while still visualizing your intentions, I want you to say to your inner world and truly feel these words:

"That or better, in divine timing and divine order, and make it easy!"

Allow these words to resonate deeply within you. Let them flow with trust and ease, knowing that everything will unfold at the perfect time in the perfect way.

Now, let it go. Go about your day, focusing on the relationships and tasks you need to attend to without constantly thinking about the intentions. When you say, "That or better," you are telling the universe that while you may have a specific desire, you're open to receiving something even better, something that aligns with your highest and best good. Trust that whatever unfolds will be in your favor and that divine timing will take care of the rest.

As we've discussed before, we do not attract what we desire, we attract what we are. The way to truly change our world is by embodying the qualities we want to manifest. For instance, if you're experiencing financial struggles, start by maintaining the feeling of what it would be like if you were not in that situation. How would you feel if you had more than enough money in your bank account— money to cover your expenses, savings, entertainment, travel, and more? Would it bring a sense of security, safety, or perhaps contentment? That's the feeling you want to cultivate.

Here's why. When you're in panic mode, whether about money or anything else, you're triggering your fight-or-flight response, which is controlled by the amygdala—the "reptilian brain." In this state, you're not functioning in your higher brain, which allows for proactive and rational decisions. Instead, you'll make impulsive choices that could potentially create more problems in the long term.

By shifting your energy, relaxing, and smoothing out your current state, you activate your higher brain functions, enabling you to make decisions that help change your physical circumstances. This shift also changes how you perceive the world and the energy around you. Remember, like attracts like. By embodying the feelings and energy of what you want, you'll attract different people, experiences, and opportunities. The universe will align with your new energy, bringing you what you desire—but on a much higher level—because you'll begin to embody what you're trying to manifest.

In other words, you will start becoming the person you want to be. This concept is reflected in the timeless sayings such as "Become the change you want to see in the world" and "You have to operate at the level you want to reach as if you are already there."

This principle was taught to me many years ago by a mentor at work. I aspired to become a training manager, a higher-profile role that involved working with executives and senior managers. My mentor advised me to act as though I was already in that position. She encouraged me to dress the part, speak the part, and do the necessary homework to prepare for any interaction with high-level executives. In essence, she taught me to perform at the level expected of someone in that role, ensuring that my work met the high standards required for that position.

This principle can be applied to any area of your life. If you want to become healthier, start by acting and living like a healthy person. If you're seeking romance, treat yourself as though you are already loved because true love begins within.

Like many others, I didn't fully understand this concept until I began examining where I was emotionally and how I viewed myself. This is why I've spent so much time in this book discussing topics that promote self-awareness. When you truly get to know yourself, you begin to see how you really view yourself.

When my mentor first gave me the advice I mentioned earlier, I remember thinking, "I can't wait! I want what I want now!" This was because I wasn't happy with where I was, and as a result, my unhappiness kept me trapped in a cycle of frustration, rather than in the forward momentum of continuous growth and development.

However, when we start to change how we see ourselves, our inner world begins to shift. And when our inner world shifts, the external world around us changes as well. We start to see conversations differently, view ourselves differently, and perceive the people around us differently. Ultimately, we attract a different life.

The key to manifesting your desires is to live as though you are already there by changing how you feel about yourself, setting your intentions, and acting as if those desires are already fulfilled all while remaining grounded in gratitude for where you are right now.

Integrating the Sovereign Mindset into Daily Life

I was inspired to write this book because I noticed a pattern in both myself and my clients while working with them. There was a significant difference in how we responded to the world around us as we did our inner work. Consistently, I observed both myself and my clients transforming how we were being (and how we responded) to life. As we made these shifts, I noticed a remarkable transformation in what some might call our "luck."

At that point, I had been meditating primarily to calm my anxiety and find some peace in my life. What I came to understand, however, was that this practice was doing much more than just helping me manage stress; it was unlocking a deeper shift in how I viewed and interacted with the world, opening doors to new opportunities and experiences.

Eventually, I began to pay more attention to how I was responding to the world. This shift wasn't just due to meditation; it was also because I had started reading about emotional intelligence, the energy body, and how it expands into vibrant, bright energy that surrounds you when fully aligned. Along with many other books and teachings, I began to understand how I fit into this world. This was exactly what I had been striving for, which was getting to know who I was and how I fit into the world, especially since I had always felt like an outcast.

As I continued this journey, I started to realize that it was my own insecurity, self-doubt, and limiting beliefs that were holding me back from my full potential. This became evident as I found myself settling for things that were not fully aligned with where I was in my life. I would settle for relationships that lacked full engagement, romantic partners who were emotionally unavailable, emotionally abusive, or simply didn't share the same feelings I did. I settled for jobs that were far beneath my capabilities—jobs that bored me but felt safe.

Does this sound familiar you?

This is why I've asked the questions I have throughout this book. As you become more self-aware of everything related to your body, mind, and soul, you will start to realize that when you live in alignment with your truth, your energy body becomes fully balanced and shines brightly. As a result, you will begin to see a world that responds to you with positive and amazing outcomes.

We spend a lifetime hearing from people who say we can do anything we set our minds to when we're younger, and then another group tells us we need to be practical. Well-intended people share many wonderful quotes and snippets of wisdom but they often aren't practicing what they're trying to teach us. This is because we're filled with ideas of instant gratification yet most people lack the stamina to push forward when things get tough. And this work can be tough. Digging into who you are and why you do the things you do is like navigating through a seemingly never-ending maze. This is why we do our inner work—to peel back the layers and discover what is truly authentic for us. The truth really does set us free, bringing freedom from confusion, struggle, and the daily anxieties of uncertainty. This is because we learn to have faith in who we are in relation to the divine aspect of ourselves on all levels.

What many of us don't understand is who we truly are on a divine level. As we get quiet, our soul will guide us to a greater understanding of who we are and who we've been avoiding while searching outside of ourselves for happiness.

I'm here to tell you that you are so much more than you think you are. You are far beyond anything your physical mind can comprehend. With that said, you can do just about anything you set your mind to.

There is a balance and a practice that keeps us grounded in the physical while also connected to Source—the universal life force. When we are connected to Source, grounded in the physical, and balanced between both, we gain the clarity we need to navigate life.

This means making healthy decisions for our physical lives and bodies while knowing that all is taken care of by the highest aspects of ourselves as we move forward into the unknown. When we balance both, we enter a state of flow where the world just seems to fall into place around us at the right time.

I have always referred to this as "dancing with God." As I move forward and allow God to guide me, I know that if God leads, I may be swung down to avoid something major, much like a partner would swing their dance partner around in a ballroom-style dance. God will fill me with strength as I approach tough terrain. It also means that God will inspire me at the right and perfect time, guiding me in my work. God will hand me passion, joy, and happiness as I align my body, mind, and soul. As I do that, I step into my sovereignty as a divine being and a child of the great God (aka Source).

This is where so many of us get stuck—and it's where I got stuck, too. When we hear the word God, we've been conditioned to think of God as separate from us. Even though most people acknowledge that the temple of God is within us, there's often a lingering feeling that God is apart from us. It's this sense of separation that blocks our access to abundance.

Even on an intellectual level, you might say, "I am one with God," or "I am an aspect of God," and yet still feel disconnected. That feeling often surfaces when it seems like something is holding you back from your dreams or when it feels as if the universe is keeping your desires from you until you're ready.

The truth is, if you feel blocked, it's not the universe—it's a part of you that still feels separate. Natural law shows us that we cannot receive what we desire until we are a vibrational match for it. It works within the energetic framework of where we are right now, guiding us to align with our highest good before our dreams can manifest.

The truth is, we are already abundant, and there is plenty of what we need for all of us because we are all children of God. The lesson is that our abundance comes from a source we are a part of, and we must access this abundance through the natural laws of the universe, which we discussed earlier in this book.

This is why the acronym "E.G.O." stands for "Edging God Out" because our EGO often demands what it wants, like a spoiled child, without understanding that we receive what we need in divine timing. We must never go against the divine order or plan as this plan is governed by natural law. That said, our EGO does serve an important purpose in our lives, which is why maintaining balance is essential for us to thrive.

It's important to remember that we don't want to eliminate the EGO entirely because it serves as a guide in the physical world. It's the part of us that tells us not to touch a hot stove or walk in front of a moving truck. A healthy EGO helps us navigate the world safely. However, an unhealthy EGO can lash out and lead to harmful actions toward ourselves and others.

When we are not in balance, we can miss important cues that we need to catch before they turn into big problems in our lives. One might ask: "This is easier said than done. How do I do this? How do I follow this inner soulful voice? How do I avoid missing it?"

The answer is practice—practice, practice, practice—and being okay with your mistakes because those mistakes are how you're going to learn. The dance with God also takes practice, much like two dance partners dancing together for the first time or a relationship that builds over time. This is done through building trust, and by building trust, sometimes things happen that hurt, make us look deeper within ourselves, and help us grow. As we grow, the dance becomes smoother, with fewer mishaps. This is because you begin to listen to your inner guidance more than outside influences.

When you are dancing with a partner and both of you are moving together, it's not just about trust with that person, it's also about trust with yourself. The more inner work you do on yourself, the fewer distractions and doubts you will have, allowing you to be fully present in the moment with that person. This is much like working with the universe (or God)—the more you do your inner work, the less doubt and distraction you experience, and the more you build trust with that higher aspect of yourself.

The more trust you have, the smoother and more enjoyable life will become. This is because you will let go of expectations and simply enjoy the moments as they come. This is also why your relationships will become much more fulfilling, as you will be fully engaged with those you love, without worrying about what will happen next or thinking about anything other than what you are doing at that moment. Being present in the moment is a key component of living in the sovereign mindset.

Peace doesn't come from having everything perfect. It comes from understanding that things unfold as they do, and peace arises from knowing that everything will be okay in the end. Even in troubling times, we know that "this too shall pass." How we show up in the world determines how we find peace within ourselves. Peace is not found outside of us; it's found within through the gradual building of inner trust. As the pendulum swings one way, we listen and remain mindful of our steps, allowing the dance to happen. As it swings the other way, we do the same until we find peace and trust in the process.

Each time we approach uncharted territory in our lives, challenges will arise, and fear may surface. That's okay. We give ourselves grace as we navigate these uncharted waters, knowing that there is a force guiding us through the unknown. Through this, we will alchemize the new venture into trust and a deeper understanding of our higher purpose and awareness of our souls and ultimately living with our sovereignty.

Another thing I have discovered is that as humans, we often get too caught up in words—and this is not where we find the deepest parts of ourselves. We find those parts through our feelings and deeper levels of our consciousness. This is deep work, and if we focus solely on words, we miss what is happening on a deeper level. Entire arguments and even churches have been founded on the literal interpretation of the Bible, even though the Bible itself emphasizes the spirit over the letter.

For example:

- **2 Corinthians 3:6 states:** *"He has made us competent as ministers of a new covenant—not of the letter but of the Spirit; for the letter kills, but the Spirit gives life."*

Other scriptures reinforce this principle:

- **Psalms 78:2** – *"I will open my mouth with a parable; I will utter hidden things, things from of old."*

This shows that while study is important, the deeper understanding of scripture comes through meditation, prayer, and practice. By engaging in these practices, we quiet our energy enough to perceive the hidden meanings, not only in the Bible but in other spiritual texts as well. Reading scripture only at the literal level causes us to miss its essence or spirit—understanding comes from experiencing life in ways like those of the original writers.

- **Proverbs 25:2** – *"It is the glory of God to conceal a thing, but the honor of kings is to search out a matter."*

This book embodies this principle: as we do our inner work, we discover our own sovereignty. We can only do this through prayer, meditation, and practice because our inner world is the realm of our divine royal selves.

These are just a few examples of scripture that encourage us to understand the Bible in a spiritual sense rather than strictly literal. Yet, in our world, we are often told to follow the letter of the law and conform to the social rules and norms of others. We could expand endlessly on this topic, but this book is not the place for that conversation. My intention is to guide you toward the authentic parts of yourself and provide a starting point for living a life in true alignment with your body, mind, and soul.

These rules we try to conform to prevent us from blossoming into our full potential. While we fear not finding our place in the world, losing family, friendships, or relationships, or falling behind in life, we limit the part of ourselves that is meant to shine brightly in the world. When that part of ourselves shines fully, the world begins to align for us, and our divine plans start to unfold, blessing us with more than we could have ever imagined.

The true awakening comes when we realize we have been settling for things that were not only outside of our divine plan but also outside the frequency at which we were meant to operate. This is not to say that you are better than anyone or anything else; it simply means that you deserve to have people, situations, and experiences in your life that match and flow with your energy. Much like the dance we discussed in this chapter, you do not want energy that weighs you down or holds you back from blossoming or operating fully within your sovereign mindset.

This is where the questions become a mirror to your soul:

- In which areas of your life do you feel constrained or held back?
- Where have you allowed the expectations, beliefs, or judgments of others to dim your light and limit your true potential?
- Do you wake each morning with a sense of vitality, fully ready to embrace the gift of this day?
- What fears, doubts, or distractions keep you from feeling truly alive and aligned with your highest self?

Let's look at these questions.

In which areas of your life do you feel constrained or held back?

Once you've identified the areas where you feel constrained or out of balance, the next step is to take deliberate action to realign yourself with your highest and best good.

Begin by asking yourself:

- What beliefs, habits, or patterns am I holding onto that no longer serve me?
- Where in my life have, I settled for less than what I truly deserve?
- What steps can I take today to move closer to alignment with my authentic self?

This process requires honesty, courage, and self-compassion. You may uncover truths about yourself that feel uncomfortable or even painful, but this is where growth happens. Each time you examine your life with clarity and presence, you create space for transformation.

Start small. Make conscious choices that reflect your true values, even in the little things. Speak your truth, set healthy boundaries, and allow yourself to say "no" when something no longer supports your growth. Over time, these small actions compound, creating profound shifts in your relationships, your work, and your overall sense of fulfillment.

Remember, this journey is not about perfection; it's about progress. It's about learning to trust yourself, your inner guidance, and the divine flow that surrounds you. As you continue to do your inner work, you will notice the dance of life becoming more graceful. The obstacles that once felt insurmountable will now feel like opportunities to practice patience, faith, and discernment.

Your Sovereign Mindset is not just a way of thinking—it's a way of being. It means living in alignment with your body, mind, and soul, and trusting that the universe—God, Source, the Divine, whatever name you give to the energy we are all a part of—supports you every step of the way. The more you cultivate this inner trust, the more effortless life becomes, and the more brightly you shine in your unique expression.

This is the essence of sovereignty: showing up fully as yourself, releasing what no longer serves you, and stepping into a life of authenticity, joy, and freedom.

Our next question is .... Where have you allowed the expectations, beliefs, or judgments of others to dim your light and limit your true potential?

We've touched on this throughout the book but it's worth revisiting because it's a deep question. When we really reflect, we realize that interactions and moments from our past have shaped how we respond to life today.

One example from my own life happened when I was six years old. My mother, cousin, and I were moving into a new apartment in Marion, Illinois. I remember most of the day but one moment stands out vividly. My mother—who almost never got upset—said to me, *"Why are you being such a little jerk today?"*

Keep in mind, parents are human. My mother was a young mother who had me at 16, so she would have been in her early twenties. And, truthfully, I probably was acting like a little jerk that day—after all, I was six years old.

The point of this story isn't about assigning blame or judging what was right or wrong. The point is about how I held onto that moment until my mid-30s. During a deep meditation, I asked myself to revisit a point in my life that was blocking my personal development. That memory came to mind.

As I peeled back the layers, I realized I was upset because I had disappointed my mother—and not upsetting her had always been very important to me. Over the years, this feeling manifested in subtle ways. Every time my mother asked me to do something, I would get defensive. Each time I got defensive, I felt like I had disappointed her. This was a subconscious response that had been building since that moment when I was six.

Nearly 30 years later, I shared this memory with my mother. She was surprised, apologetic, and honestly didn't even remember the moment. In giving myself grace, I had to recognize that I was a six-year-old boy at the time, and much of my reaction had been based on a child's perception. This became a moment for growth in my life. As I processed it and healed, my relationship with my mother deepened and became even closer. This is why it's so important to express our feelings. By doing so, we can heal misunderstandings, release old patterns, and align more fully with our souls. When we address these subconscious blocks, we reclaim our light and open ourselves to our true potential.

Our next question is ... Do you wake each morning with a sense of vitality, fully ready to embrace the gift of this day?

This is one of those yes-or-no questions—and that's intentional. You either wake up with this sense of vitality and readiness or you do not. I realize some of you may think it's more complicated than a simple yes or no, and I want to push back on that. No, it's not complicated. You either are fully present and energized for the day or you are not.

You might be wondering why I'm being so rigid with this question. The reason is simple: when you're exploring deep questions like this, you need clarity. Anything other than a direct yes or no answer usually indicates that you are avoiding the truth. Excuses, explanations, and long-winded stories can easily get in the way of uncovering what's really holding you back.

For example, when I work with someone in a troubled marriage, I often hear explanations about why their spouse is disconnected or disengaged. Maybe the spouse is unhappy due to communication breakdowns, misunderstandings, or simply because they are no longer a match. And while action may be needed in the relationship, the tendency is for people to get caught up in explaining the situation rather than identifying the root issue. They are avoiding the deeper question: why am I not feeling a sense of vitality in my life? Why don't I see each day as a gift?

So, let's go deep on this one. We want to clear the thoughts, feelings, and energy that prevent you from living your optimal life. By answering honestly, without excuses, you begin to uncover the blocks that are keeping you from embracing each day with fullness, joy, and purpose.

Our last question of these four is ... What fears, doubts, or distractions keep you from feeling truly alive and aligned with your highest self?

I am sure all of us have struggled with fears, doubts, and distractions. How they manifest in our lives can differ based on who we are, our circumstances, and several other factors. By asking these questions, however, we get to explore a deeper sense of ourselves. This was something I had to look at closely as I finished my college education. When I reflected on the fact that it took me 30 years to complete college, it was eye opening. Part of this was because I had no clear idea of what I wanted to do when I "grew up." I eventually discovered a path in Learning and Development, which opened me to my own self-development. When I integrated my spiritual life with my career, it became clear that I wanted to pursue leadership in Learning and Development and earn a master's degree in adult education.

I was fascinated by virtual learning and its ability to reach people all over the world. I had also always been intrigued by social media and its power to both help and harm people. Finally having direction was just the first step—then came the work on myself: confronting the excuses, distractions, doubts, and insecurities that arose with this path.

This is why it took me nearly 20 years to complete my bachelor's degree and master's degree. While working on these degrees during COVID, I noticed the same energies of procrastination and self-doubt resurfacing when I tackled assignments. I had to push myself harder because now I was investing my own money and effort, fully aware that completing this degree would transform my life.

When something is truly important—and you know that if you don't do it now, you may never do it—you tend to push harder. Excuses lose their power in the face of a deep desire to fulfill your purpose. Through the act of completion, your energy transforms. Achieving something you've worked tirelessly for elevates your self-respect and reshapes how you see yourself.

When you look in the mirror after such accomplishments, you see a new reflection staring back—one filled with strength, love, and gratitude. You begin to love yourself more deeply and honor not just the destination, but the entire journey that brought you here.

This is why effort is essential—not only in pursuing our dreams but in our healing and personal growth. The work we put in shapes our energy, our self-perception, and ultimately, the life we can live.

As you can probably imagine, who I am and what I dreamed of being 20 years ago has evolved over time. Like many of us, through my experiences, I have developed a deeper understanding of who I am as an individual. This is why life is about the journey, not necessarily the destination.

For you, the reader, this means giving yourself grace. You will set goals and experience setbacks. You will make mistakes, stumble, and celebrate successes. You will take leaps of faith, only to feel terrified and retreat to the safety of your comfort zone. Yet, you will stand back up, get on that metaphorical bike, and ride forward again. When you fall, you might try to convince yourself it was a mistake but I can guarantee there will be a part of you that wants to get back on that bike and ride because there is a part of you yearning to be free, to stand in your own power, and to feel fully alive.

That is the part of you we want to nurture, develop, and eventually allow to soar. Living with a sovereign mindset is your path to freedom—your path to finally living authentically, fully engaged with yourself, and cultivating a loving, empowering relationship with your own life.

CHAPTER

11

Real-Life Transformations

I want to be clear. While I share my stories—and the stories of others—this book is also about you. Many of you have lived through experiences like these, and even if you haven't, my stories are still yours. We all face challenges, and it is through those challenges that we discover our strength, our resilience, and who we truly are.

This book is meant to guide you inward, to help you see your full potential, and to remind you that there is a part of you which, when aligned, opens the door to a life overflowing with experiences, miracles, surprises, and joy—a life fully enriched with possibilities.

Let me leave you with one story before we dive into more stories. In 2003, my mother's best friend visited me in Virginia Beach and said, *"Jeremy, one thing you do is 'long' for things. It's okay to have wishes and dreams, but your desire is so strong that you no longer live in the present moment or enjoy it for what it is."*

Almost 20 years later, in December 2021, I heard that message again in a dream. Around the same time, I reflected on one of the Ten Commandments, "Thou shalt not covet." To covet means to long for something that is not yours. When you covet, when you look at someone else's life wishing it were yours, you are not in alignment with your own life. Your energy is elsewhere, and manifestation always happens in the present moment based on the frequency you are vibrating right now.

Gratitude for this moment—right here, right now—is essential. If your mind is too far in the future, you're not truly living today. As someone once said to me, 'When you've got one foot in tomorrow and one foot in yesterday, you're pissing on today.' At the time, I laughed, because to my 20-year-old self, it sounded funny. But looking back, I realized it was actually a very wise statement.

As you read these stories, see them as mirrors for your own life. The circumstances may differ, but the lessons are universal. You've all had moments of clarity—times when life flowed, when doors opened, and when miracles seemed possible. Those moments are proof of the energy you can access when you align with yourself. That is the energy I want you to tune into as you continue this journey.

Some of these stories are hard to hear, but I want you to see the truth in them. Even when people make mistakes, even when they go through some of the darkest, most challenging times in their lives, they can step into a completely new life. In some cases, the "old" version of themselves dies, making way for someone who is full of life, understanding, and alignment with their soul's purpose. Miracles can and do happen along the way but the true shift comes when a person fully aligns with who they are on a soul level. When that happens, the world begins to move in their favor.

My first story is a powerful one. It's about a woman who, in 1988, was sentenced to a 90-year prison term for drug trafficking but was released in just over 20 years. What makes her story so inspiring is not just the sentence she endured but the incredible personal and spiritual growth she experienced while in prison.

From the very beginning, she told the judge, "You'll see me again," knowing she would not be in prison forever. And she meant it. Once inside, she immersed herself in the community, began tutoring others, and eventually became a paralegal. She dedicated herself to self-improvement, reading books on personal development and learning how to incorporate spirituality into her daily life. Without even realizing it, she was changing as a person, focusing on her growth rather than dwelling on her circumstances. She told me in our interview that going to prison had been one of the best things that ever happened to her although it may seem odd to most because it pushed her to grow personally and spiritually.

She never gave up on coming home. She filed motions, hired attorneys, and pursued every opportunity, but the door seemed perpetually closed. In her sixth year, two undercover detectives, during their investigations, kept encountering her name. They couldn't believe she had received a 90-year sentence. While they knew she had to serve time, 90 years felt excessive, so they filed a motion on her behalf. A few weeks later, she returned to court before the same judge, who reduced her sentence to 35 years. It was still a long time but compared to 90, it was a gift. This was the universe preparing her for what was to come, giving her a glimmer of hope at the end of the tunnel.

Back in prison, she again immersed herself in the community, this time starting a youth group for girls. By her 20th year, she was mentally and emotionally exhausted. Like she did every day, she prayed, and this time she said, "God, I am tired, and I am so ready to go home. I think I have done everything I can do here, and I am ready to come home." In our interview, she shared that a voice spoke to her and said: "File for clemency." And that's exactly what she did.

The clemency process is a complex and challenging task. Because you are not present for a hearing, everything must be put on paper—

precisely, compellingly, and with complete honesty. Many women spend years on this process, struggling to bare their deepest truths. At first, she couldn't even begin but once she let go of control, she completed her petition in just two weeks, telling me that it didn't even feel like she was the one writing it. Her parents were overjoyed, and along the way, people unexpectedly appeared in their lives to support her efforts.

Through it all, her faith remained unwavering. She knew, without a doubt, that she was coming home and even knew the exact date: December 10, 2010—exactly 22 years after her sentencing. That year was an election year in Florida, and her first hearing was postponed. Still, she remained certain she was returning home. On December 9, the clemency board finally met. Her parents organized a Greyhound bus filled with supporters—people she didn't even know to represent her in Tallahassee—church members, colleagues of her father from the police department, and others who believed in her cause.

She emphasized to me that throughout this journey, immersing herself fully in faith was essential. The world would try to distract her, challenge her beliefs, and sow doubt but holding onto faith gave her strength. On the day of the hearing, she ate lunch alone—clemencies are difficult, and many applicants, even those with perfect records, are denied. Despite this, she kept her focus on her faith and kept her eyes on the prize.

Then, the moment arrived. She heard her name called, left her food tray, and walked with the guard to the administrative building. She knew she was going home. She had even begun giving her belongings away to other inmates in anticipation. The warden finally told her that she was going home—on December 10, 2010.

Her story is a testament to the power of perseverance, faith, and personal transformation. Even in the darkest circumstances, miracles are possible. By focusing on her growth, embracing spirituality, and fully immersing herself in faith, she aligned with her true self—and in doing so, she allowed the universe to move on her behalf. One of the most inspiring parts of her story is what she did after her release. She helped people leaving prison find jobs and adapt to life outside. She reached out to employers to create opportunities for convicted felons, helping them reintegrate into their communities, raise their energy, and build fulfilling lives. Not only did she transform her own life, but she also became a source of healing and inspiration for countless others.

When she shared her story with me, I was overwhelmed by its power. When I outlined this book, I initially wondered if I had other stories to tell besides my own. A week later, there she was, sitting in front of me, sharing her journey. From that moment, I realized that people with remarkable stories would come into my life naturally. One thing is certain—when you set clear intentions, the energy moves in your favor. The universe aligns to bring the opportunities, connections, and circumstances that you need to succeed and to remind you of the resources and resilience you already possess.

This brings me to another story, equally powerful but in a very different way. It centers on a woman who had endured years of depression and the effects of a severe brain injury. Despite seeking help from the medical community, she received no answers. The weight of despair became unbearable, and she reached a point where she no longer wanted to live. She researched ways to end her life and ultimately decided to jump from the Skyway Bridge in Tampa Bay, Florida. One morning, at 7:30 a.m., she drove to the bridge and leapt.

What followed was nothing short of miraculous. During her 19-story fall, she blacked out, only regaining consciousness inches above the water. By an extraordinary twist of fate, she landed just 20 feet from a charter boat with four trauma specialists on board. They rescued her and ensured she reached the hospital safely. According to unofficial records, of the 366 "jumpers" from the Skyway Bridge, 317 died, and only 49 survived. Her survival alone was a miracle but what makes her story truly remarkable is what happened next.

In that life-altering moment, she made a powerful declaration to herself: "I want to live." By stating her intention so clearly, she aligned herself with the universe, which responded in kind. This moment became the turning point that shifted the trajectory of her life. From that day forward, she committed herself to healing, personal growth, and helping others in her community who were struggling. She transformed her pain into purpose, using her experience to inspire and uplift those around her.

Both these stories show a common truth: when we align with our true desires, immerse ourselves in faith, and focus on personal transformation, life has a way of responding to us in miraculous ways. The universe conspires in our favor, opportunities appear, and even the most challenging circumstances can become a catalyst for growth. These stories are not just about the individuals in them— they are a mirror for all of us. They are reminders that no matter where we are, no matter how dark our path seems, the power to change our lives, to heal, and to step fully into our potential has always been within us.

Stories like these are ones we hear often, and many times they become movies or books that inspire us because we can relate to the pain and challenges they show. Yet the real challenge lies in our own belief in ourselves. It's difficult to truly know ourselves on a deep, soulful level because we are so caught up in the expectations of the world and the codependent patterns we've been taught from an early age. We are rarely quiet or still enough to develop the relationship with ourselves that are necessary to create real healing and lasting positive change in our lives.

This leads me to my next story about a woman who has not only helped me but has helped heal countless others. Like all of us who guide others, she first had to heal herself. Before her journey of transformation, she was an award-winning Catholic educator who had shaped young minds for many years. She had been married for 29 years and had two children.

One day, she experienced a massive heart attack and was rushed to the hospital. During this medical episode, she had what we would call a near-death experience—she went straight up and met God before returning to her body. This encounter changed everything. The way she saw, felt, and experienced the world shifted so profoundly that her husband urged her to return to the hospital to regain the person she had been before the heart attack but it was too late. She had already changed. She could not go back because she realized that, until that moment, she had never fully lived her life.

As you can imagine, her entire life transformed. She began to explore an incredible phenomena unfolding around her since her near-death experience—she discovered her true self on a much deeper level. Naturally, as she changed, the world around her changed. People in her life shifted. Some left entirely. Transformation, she learned, changes the very landscape of your life.

As you shed the layers of the masks we all wear for the world, you begin to see the illusions that surround us—and beyond them, a world far greater and more profound than anything we could have imagined. As she started truly seeing who she was on a soulful level, she began sharing the lessons she was learning with others. She understood that by continuing her own inner work, she would receive the tools to help guide those ready to heal, and this became her life's work, a mission she continues to this day. By helping people peel back the layers of their lives and embrace their true selves, she was healing families and communities because as others did their own inner work, their transformation inspired more healing around them.

The last story I want to share is about someone I have known for years. Without going into all the details, their past was filled with trauma, which made them hesitant to fully open their heart to anyone and afraid of what that vulnerability might bring. Their healing journey began in 2012, after a fall that triggered a profound energy shift lasting roughly 24 hours. During that time, they experienced complete clarity about life, realizing that many of their fears and worries were not as overwhelming as they had imagined. I remember standing beside them, feeling the intensity of their energy. It was so powerful that it was almost difficult for me to concentrate.

During this 24-hour period, they saw shadows and images that resembled ghosts—some with red eyes, others mere dark silhouettes. This clarity shifted the way they perceived the world although the most profound transformation would come years later, in 2017. That year, they collapsed at home from a seizure and were rushed to the hospital where doctors discovered that fluid was not draining properly from their brain. The pressure was affecting their frontal lobe, and they were told they would need surgery or risk death. They chose to have the operation, and on the day of the surgery, they experienced an out-of-body moment, feeling as though they were hovering above their body.

Throughout the month-long hospital stay, their partner never left their side. This unwavering support allowed them to finally open their heart—not only to their partner but also to those who truly cared for them. They began to embrace vulnerability, committing to their own healing in ways they never had before. In this process, they learned powerful lessons about control: while some things in life are beyond our influence, the connections we nurture with those we love are profoundly shaped by simply showing up as our authentic selves.

As the author of this book, I have had the privilege of witnessing their transformation over the years. Observing their growth has inspired me on my own journey. One of the most profound gifts of friendship is seeing those we love evolve while providing them with the space and support to fully become who they are meant to be.

These stories have inspired me, and it is my hope that they have inspired you to look in the mirror and recognize that we all have our crosses to bear, so to speak. Yet, there is always the opportunity to transform your life into one filled with inspiration, fulfillment, connection, and love.

I know these stories might seem extreme but I am here to tell you that we all have moments when hope feels lost, when we feel unheard, unseen, undervalued, or unloved. What I want you to understand is that all those things—hope, love, value—have always been within you. The stories I shared are about people who faced some of the hardest moments in life. As they finally let go, the universe began to show them that they were never alone; in fact, the universe was conspiring to do them good.

And this is exactly what I want you to see for yourself. Their journeys weren't about luck, favoritism, or external circumstances; they were about alignment, inner work, and trusting the process. When you fully invest in yourself, embrace your sovereign mindset, and build a relationship with your own soul, you open the door for life to flow in ways you may have never imagined. You don't need anyone else's approval, a perfect plan, or a guaranteed path. The miracle is already within you, waiting for you to step into it.

Ask yourself—are you willing to do the inner work, trust your own growth, and say yes to the life that's waiting for you? I sincerely hope so.

The Journey
Continues

12

I have mentioned this throughout the book but the process of understanding yourself is a lifelong journey. When we embrace the attitude of lifelong learning, we begin to truly change how we see the world. The idea that we can learn something once, fully understand it, and never need to revisit it is a misconception reinforced by society. This mindset creates the expectation that once a lesson has been presented to us, we will never make a mistake because we've learned the lesson or that we won't ever need to revisit the lesson.

The best way to understand that misguided concept is by considering a book or a movie you've read or watched again. Don't you find that as time has passed, that you understand new things or have a different perspective upon the second viewing or second reading? Haven't you ever had a new or a different appreciation for a certain character than you did upon your first read? Don't you sometimes notice new things about the set or the dialogue that you didn't pick up on during your first viewing? The tendency to view things with a new lens is exactly why we are better off if we revisit lessons we only thought we learned in years past. That's not to say we didn't learn it properly the first time; it's merely to suggest that each reading/viewing is another opportunity to learn new lessons and gain a different or greater understanding of something.

I've noticed this pattern often while working with clients. I would bring up an area for growth, only to hear, "I already worked on this years ago." One instance that stands out is a female client I was speaking with about inner child work. Before I could even explain, she blurted out, "No, I worked on my inner child 10 years ago!" Just by the way she reacted, I could tell there was still work to be done but at that moment, she wasn't ready to hear it. A few years later, she returned to me and admitted she needed to revisit her inner child work, exactly as I had suggested before. This experience was a powerful reminder that true growth isn't linear, and sometimes the lessons we think we've mastered require us to come back to them with new awareness and a different perspective to get a deeper understanding.

I want to share this topic from both my background in education and the lessons life has taught me along the way. Before we dive in, let's revisit a powerful concept we've touched on before—**divine timing and divine order**. This idea doesn't just apply to spirituality; it also mirrors the way we learn, grow, and adapt throughout our lives.

Think about the process of learning something new. Whenever we do, our brain begins to build a fresh neural pathway. But here's the thing—it doesn't happen all at once. Until that pathway fully connects, we're essentially walking in faith. We take one step at a time, trusting that the pieces will come together, even when they don't make sense yet.

A great example of this is learning how to drive. Remember those early days behind the wheel? You probably checked every mirror twice, gripped the steering wheel at ten and two, and carefully followed each instruction you were taught. It felt overwhelming at first, but then—almost without realizing it—you crossed a threshold. One day, you got in the car, started the engine, and drove without thinking about every little step. That moment was proof that your brain had connected the pathway. Driving was now second nature.

Now here's where it gets tricky, especially for adults. If we can't see how a new idea, skill, or practice is going to make a difference in our lives, our brain tends to resist it. And when it comes to spiritual concepts—things like faith, trust, or surrender—they can feel even harder to grasp. Why? Because they often require time, patience, and consistency, and for many of us, that feels like it takes us away from the "real" demands of life—family, finances, careers, and responsibilities.

You've probably heard spiritual teachers talk about faith, and it's true—faith is essential. But the human mind also needs a reason. It wants to understand why taking these steps will matter, why the effort is worth it, and what will ultimately change.

That's why I always remind people to give themselves grace on their journey. Lifelong learning, whether in the classroom or on the spiritual path, isn't about instant results. It's about honoring the process, trusting that each step forward is part of divine timing, and allowing your growth to unfold in its own perfect order.

When we talk about divine timing and divine order, I can't help but connect it to the way both children and adults learn. We rarely absorb something all at once—it usually comes in small, bite-sized pieces of information and experience. True learning unfolds gradually, often through living the lesson rather than simply hearing about it.

Think of it like planting a seed. You don't drop it in the soil and expect a fully grown tree the next morning. First comes the sprout, then the tender stem, and over time, it develops branches, leaves, and eventually fruit. Each stage is necessary. Each step, no matter how small, carries the wisdom needed for the next.

It's the same with our intentions and goals. As we set them, the universe responds by bringing us the exact lessons we need but always in manageable steps. These lessons come as small experiences, insights, or challenges, shaping us little by little. Every time we lean into those lessons, new neural pathways are formed in our brain, and with them, a new perspective.

This has been my experience in writing this book. It's one thing to speak about theory but another entirely to weave theory together with lived experience. Just like a tree that has weather seasons of sun, rain, and storms, lived experience gives theory its strength. That's when clarity emerges, and we begin to see not just how we grow as individuals, but how we evolve as souls.

This is the essence of the sovereign mindset: gathering the lessons of our lives, allowing them to take root, and transforming them into the wisdom that nourishes who we are today and then bridges the gap between the body, mind and soul.

What I've noticed with so many of my clients—and what I've spoken about throughout this book—is how easily we get weighed down by other people's ideas. We start living under the shadow of fear: fear of being judged, fear of being an outcast, fear of losing what we already have, or fear of wasting our time or our money.

I want you to pause for a moment and reflect on your own life. Think back on the journey you've walked. No doubt, there have been seasons filled with joy and others marked by struggle. But here's the real question I want you to sit with: **when you reach the end of your life, based on where you are today, will you feel that you truly lived? Will you know in your heart that you followed your soul's calling?**

Or, will you look back with regret, wondering why you didn't pursue the things you yearned to experience? One thing is certain, regret is one of the heaviest burdens we can carry. And the last thing you want at the end of your journey is to look back and wish you had done something different.

Many of the concepts I've shared may sound simple on the surface. Some of you might be thinking, *"This sounds easy—I've got this."* Others may feel the opposite, thinking, *"This is going to be really hard."* The truth is, both reactions are normal. What matters most is remembering that you don't have to walk this journey alone.

We all need community. At the very least, you need one trusted person you can talk to—someone you can process your experiences with as they come up. Because they will come up. And often, we can't see everything clearly on our own. That's why community is so powerful. It helps us notice our blind spots, move through roadblocks, and mirror back insights that we might otherwise miss.

I've even given my own community permission to do this for me. I remember a time when my heart was broken. A close friend comforted me but also gently pointed out something I hadn't wanted to see—that I had overlooked red flags that had been there all along. He wasn't trying to hurt me; he was helping me recognize a truth I needed to face so that I could grow from the experience.

And that's what community does. It helps us process, reflect, and gain clarity. Each experience, even the painful ones, are an opportunity for growth. And growth is what brings us closer to our soul, aligning our body, mind, and spirit. That alignment is what allows us to live and operate with a sovereign mind.

I can tell you this: there will be days you struggle. Days you don't like life. Days when you may even question why you're here on this planet at all. And yet, all of it is part of the journey. As the saying goes, it's less about the destination and more about the journey itself.

One of the most powerful stories I've ever heard that captures this truth came from a woman named Jenn Drummond, a mountaineer who has climbed Mount Everest as well as the Seven Second Summits on all seven continents. When she tells her story about Everest, it makes you stop and reflect on your own life.

Her journey began when her child challenged her to climb Mount Everest. She trained for countless hours, pushing herself physically, emotionally, and mentally. She describes the mountain howling as snowdrifts shifted beneath her feet and the moment she crossed a ladder spanning a gorge that dropped more than a mile below. Finally, she reached the summit where she had just 10 minutes to take a photo with her flag before turning back so she'd have enough oxygen to descend safely.

Listening to her describe the climb, it became clear—the victory wasn't the 10 minutes at the summit—it was everything that came before it. The preparation. The fear. The determination. The countless hours of training that shaped not just her body but also her spirit. The climb was about discovering who she was, not simply about standing on top of the mountain. She ended her talk with a powerful question: **"What is your Everest?"**

I first heard her share this story in November 2023, as a keynote speaker for an online event I produced just before I left for Scotland and moved out of my apartment. At that time, I was standing at the base of my own Everest: relaunching the Spirit Heart Cruise, building online events, finishing this book, and stepping into this work full time. It was exhilarating and terrifying. I remember shaking with fear as I took those first steps, wondering how it could possibly come together. But step by step, the path unfolded. And I realized the universe had been preparing me all along through small lessons that built into the bigger one.

Looking back, I can see why I struggled so much after publishing my first book, **Peace Be Still.** Every challenge, every detour, every heartbreak had been God—the universe—revealing who I truly was on a deeper level. Beyond the words on the page, I was asked to live the message. And through it all, even as my community shifted and changed, a few trusted souls remained by my side—reminding me that no one climbs their Everest alone.

As you reach the final pages of this book, I want to leave you with a question: **What is your Everest?** Where in your life are you holding back? What's keeping you from experiencing life to its fullest?

One of my favorite parts of Jenn Drummond's presentation has always stayed with me because it's similar to what I ask my clients. Many people tell me they can't pursue their dreams because they have responsibilities—family, children, careers—and yes, those responsibilities are real. But Jenn's perspective adds a powerful layer of truth.

As she pursued her goal of climbing Everest (despite being afraid of heights) and the Seven Second Summits on all seven continents, she did it not only for herself but for her children. She wanted them to see that when you set a goal, you stick with it—even when it's hard. She showed them that the journey matters just as much as the destination. And through that journey, she grew as an individual while also teaching her children by example.

So, I ask you: where could you be an example to your loved ones? Too often, we give advice about things we haven't truly lived. But the most powerful lessons don't come from our words, they come from our actions. Go live it. Step into your Everest. Let your life become the lesson.

From this day forward, I encourage you to make you a priority. Work on yourself. Grow, expand, and align with your soul. When you do, I promise your life will shift in profound ways. And the people who are truly meant to walk beside you will remain by your side—not only supporting you but growing alongside you as each of you takes steps on your own sacred journey.

EPILOGUE

Your Divine Potential Awaits

One truth I've discovered is that a part of you has been patiently waiting for your recognition and for your love. This part of you whispers through the signs in your life, nudges you through intuition, and lights the way when the path seems unclear. It is woven into the fabric of consciousness, energy, and the divine—call it God, Source, or however your soul understands it. The universe is always guiding you, always orchestrating circumstances for your highest good. The key is to notice, to trust, and to open your heart to this quiet, powerful energy that is working for your growth, your joy, and your awakening.

We crave order. We want life to feel safe, predictable, and manageable. And yet, even in the moments that feel dark, uncertain, or overwhelming, there is a force guiding you—subtle, unwavering, unstoppable. These "dark nights of the soul" are not punishments—they are invitations—invitations to grow, to rise, to step fully into the power of who you are meant to be.

A friend once said to me during a hard time, "I thought spirituality was supposed to be peaceful." I smiled and said, "If it were that simple, everyone would do it." Discovering your soul, your true self, is not easy. It asks you to face yourself, your fears, and your shadows—and to rise anyway.

As you walk your path, life will shift. Relationships will fade. People will leave. They no longer resonate with the energy you are becoming—and that is okay. Each release creates space for what truly matters: clarity, purpose, joy, and a peace anchored within you—not dependent on anyone or anything outside of you. This is the path of awakening, the path of sovereignty, the path to living fully, authentically, and unapologetically.

I believe deeply that we attract exactly what we need, exactly when we need it. That means you are here, right now, reading this book, at exactly the perfect time. I wrote it through inspired action because it was my time. The energy we share—the energy of me fulfilling my purpose and you fulfilling yours by reading—confirms this: the universe is conspiring in your favor. It is time for your life to flow in alignment with your body, mind, and soul.

This journey is about fully realizing who you are on a grander scale and claiming the sovereignty that is your birthright. You are not less than. You are not lacking. You are a divine spark of the divine. You are divine royalty. Thoughts that tell you otherwise—of lack, sin, unworthiness—are illusions. Now is the day you release them.

You are abundant. You are glorious. You deserve the very best that life has to offer. I am thrilled to witness this movement grow, to see souls awaken to the greatness they were born to be—and you are a vital part of this shift. Matthew 18:20 reminds us, "For where two or three gather in my name, there am I with them." There is always a force working in your favor. As we awaken to our own divine nature, we give others permission to awaken to theirs.

This is the rhythm of the universe. As we fulfill our divine plan and operate with renewed minds, we begin to see the world works for us, not against us. Challenges arise to push us, to teach us, to guide us.

Joyful moments make our soul sing. And through it all, every experience serves the highest and best good of our soul.

Soul Alignment Exercise: Reclaiming Your Power

1. **Find Your Space:** Sit or stand somewhere quiet. Breathe deeply. Relax your body. Quiet your mind. Open your soul.

2. **Declare Your Truth:** Speak aloud, or silently:

3. "I am love. I am loved. I honor all of me—body, mind, and soul. In the highest and best good, I reclaim my power. From every person, place, and entity, from every space, portal, time, and dimension, from every connection, attachment, and vessel, I call my energy back. To anyone or anything trying to take it—I say: NO. I am whole. I am free. I am mine."

4. **Feel the Energy:** Visualize a golden light surrounding you. Filling every cell. Flowing through your mind. Expanding from your soul. Feel it reclaiming your power, restoring your energy, anchoring your sovereignty.

5. **Set Your Intention:** Connect with your highest self. Ask yourself, "How will I honor my soul today? How can I align with my highest good?" Trust the answers—your soul knows the way.

6. **Close With Gratitude:** Thank yourself, the universe, the divine—for guidance, energy, and love that is always working in your favor.

7. **Repeat Daily:** The more you commit, the stronger your energy becomes, the clearer your path, and the more your life flows in alignment with your divine nature.

Exercises like this can be simple, yet when practiced daily, they have the power to shift your energy from within and that is exactly where transformation begins. Like many of us, I once looked outward for happiness. I believed I needed money to achieve my dreams, a loving partner by my side while doing my spiritual work, or flashy cars to prove my success to the world. While those things can be enjoyable, they pale in comparison to what is possible when you work from the inside out.

Everything you think you want becomes insignificant compared to the abundance, love, and fulfillment that flow naturally when you embrace your full potential. If any of those external things are meant for you, they will come with ease and grace because you have done the inner work. The right people will enter your life, love will naturally gravitate toward you, and abundance will fall into your lap. Why? Because you have cultivated a deep relationship with the being you truly are—a child of the divine.

Why settle for anything less than all your glory? This is your moment to let go. To be vulnerable. To dive deep into the soul of who you are. Logic cannot guide you here—only your heart, only your courage. You may cry. You may have questions. You may doubt. You may wonder if it's worth it. And yet ... you will keep going. Because on the other side of this journey is you—fully awake, fully alive, fully sovereign.

I tell my students this: *you cannot logic your way into heaven.* Heaven is not made of rules, it is light. It is not weight, it is flow. When you move with your true nature, everything falls into place—even what once felt impossible.

Ask yourself ... What will it take for you to finally say yes to yourself? What will it take to make you your own priority? The love you crave is already inside. The connection you seek is already within. Your soul is waiting. Your life is waiting. So, start today. Step into your light. Step into your power. Step into you.

Connect with Jeremy E. Mcdonald

Scan the QR code or click the links below to connect with Jeremy through his website and social channels.

🌐 Website: https://www.jeremymcdonald.net

📷 Instagram: https://www.instagram.com/jeremy_e_mcdonald